empath
heart

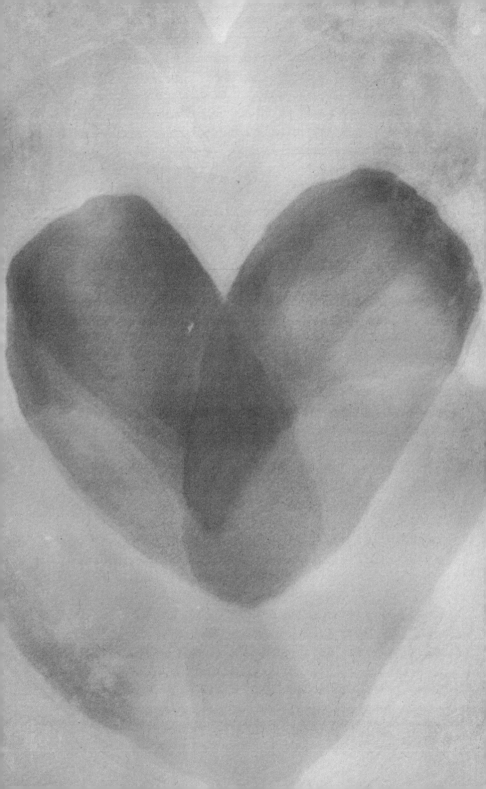

empath
heart

RELATIONSHIP
STRATEGIES
FOR SENSITIVE
PEOPLE

tanya carroll richardson

STERLING ETHOS
New York

STERLING ETHOS
New York

An Imprint of Sterling Publishing Co., Inc.

Readers are advised to consult their doctors or other qualified health-care
professionals regarding the treatment of their medical or psychological concerns.
Please note that the information in this book is not meant to diagnose, treat,
prescribe, or substitute consultation with a licensed health-care professional.

ISBN 978-1-4549-4688-5 (paperback)
ISBN 978-1-4549-4689-2 (e-book)

Library of Congress Control Number: 2022949138

For information about custom editions,
special sales, and premium purchases, please
contact specialsales@unionsquareandco.com.

Printed in Canada

2 4 6 8 10 9 7 5 3 1

unionsquareandco.com

Interior design by Christine Heun

To empaths everywhere . . .
May you use your sensitivity,
and any other graces you possess,
to make the world a better place.

To my husband, Michael . . .
Thank you for twenty years of marriage,
for your love and friendship,
and for always supporting my dreams.

Contents

Exercises & Quizzes

Introduction

Being an Empath
in Relationship with Others

Let me begin by assuring you that I do *not* have all the answers! What I can share in this book are tools that have worked for myself and for sensitive friends, family, and many of the thousands of clients all over the world who have come to me for intuitive sessions. Please take away what resonates and works best for *you*. If someone else suggests a different technique or way-of-being with sensitivity that's a better fit for your life, embrace it. Always trust yourself and your own powerful intuition for the best way to live your unique life as a sensitive person. I want only the best for you, whether that guidance comes from me, yourself, or someone else.

Empaths are hyperperceptive, meaning they pick up more easily on the energies and emotions of other individual people, the collective energies and emotions of groups, and the energies of physical spaces and objects. Some empaths are even more sensitive than most people to physical stimuli like noise and temperature changes.

Empaths are typically drawn to nature—keeping fresh-smelling flowers around the house or hanging out to meditate under a tree—because they can tune in to nature's supportive energy. Some empaths might have a special relationship with animals and be able to communicate with them intuitively. Basically, empaths feel and sense a lot!

This ability to pick up on so much around them can be a huge blessing, allowing empaths to open up and feel more connected to others and the world. An empath's unique sensitivity lets them experience life in a rich, multidimensional, immediate way. For empaths, feeling so much can be incredibly nourishing, increasing their ability to tune in to the depth of the present moment. Empaths have an ability to savor the present moment as others might savor a great dessert or a perfect cup of coffee.

Being able to feel the energies and emotions of other individuals, groups, or spaces as if those energies and emotions were an empath's own also presents challenges. Feeling everything around you in your own system means that as an empath, you can more easily become overwhelmed and overstimulated.

In my book *Self-Care for Empaths*, I concentrated on teaching empaths how to ground in to their own energy, how to manage overstimulation, how to understand their intuitive system, and how to observe and witness the world instead of always feeling everything (feeling everything is great, but it's nice to have options).

In *Empath Heart*, I'll be focusing on how to work with your empath sensitivity regarding your intimate relationships with others. Whether it's a relationship with a manager, child, close friend, romantic partner, sibling, coworker, parent, or client, this book will give you empath-specific tools to help you enjoy that relationship even more, while at the same time protecting your sensitivity more too. I'm a big believer that awareness is an amazing transformative change agent. Each section of the book will also contain a short exercise and simple mantra to help clarify the concept.

Relationships with other people provide us with some of our greatest emotional experiences, as well as some of our greatest life lessons. Yet your primary relationship is to yourself, so throughout the book we'll also be nurturing your self-love, which truly can be the greatest love of all. Great truths are often found in paradoxes; and paradoxically, strengthening your relationship to yourself can be the surest way to strengthen your relationships with others.

As a professional intuitive, I've had one-on-one sessions with thousands of empath clients all over the world. While I'll be drawing on their experiences as well as my own in this book, any information about clients will be altered significantly to protect each individual's identity. While every empath is fabulously unique, I often notice patterns that many of my sensitive clients have struggled with regarding their close relationships. So you may recognize yourself in some of these examples.

Remember that this book is *never* meant to replace working with a health-care professional, like a trained doctor or counselor. Some of the exercises in this book might do the trick for you, and others will be merely jumping-off or starting points for you. Always seek out as much support as you need—you deserve it!

Just like you have a physical body, you also have an energy body. Empaths have a very sensitive and receptive energy body. Your empath heart is a gift, an energetic marvel that allows you to feel and sense so much. I hope this book helps you better comprehend and treasure that energetic heart. Empaths have a strong natural intuition, so you'll get a lot of information in this book about using your sixth sense to help you navigate relationships too.

Your sensitivity is one of the unique things that makes you special—yet everyone is special and worthy! Friends, colleagues, and family members who are not as sensitive as you are also gloriously, equally special and worthy. This book should help you help them learn to respect, understand, work with, and honor your sensitivity.

Writing and publishing a book is a very rewarding journey, one that you, the reader, share an equal part in. Thank you for going on this journey with me!

Love from my empath heart to yours,

—*Tanya*

Chapter 1

Assertiveness for Empaths

Assertiveness—confidently and straightforwardly communicating your needs and desires to others—can be challenging for empaths. Sensitive empaths can be as strong and self-assured as anyone. Yet empaths can also feel what others want and need so easily that it can make an empath shy away from expressing their own wants and needs honestly and directly. What if an empath's wants or needs are the opposite of what their partner or manager wants and needs? That's always a tough situation, but for an empath it can be doubly so.

Because empaths feel the energies and emotions of others easily and intimately in their own systems, voicing an agenda contradictory to someone else's means an empath might very well feel the other person's sadness, anger, frustration, disappointment, or simple displeasure in their own system. It doesn't matter if the exchange is in person, on the phone, or via text and email—empaths are easily able to pick up on energy, no matter how it travels. Empaths can even *anticipate* feeling how someone else will react before they've voiced any of their own feelings or desires.

Whether you are a very compassionate empath who doesn't want to cause others to feel challenging emotions, or you are wanting to protect yourself from absorbing the challenging emotions of others—or both—this chapter is packed with tools to help you be more assertive in your everyday interactions. Expressing your wants and needs is an act of self-love that honors you and improves your life. It's also an act of grace that gives others the benefit of your authentic thoughts and feelings.

Coming Home to Yourself After Considering the Perspectives of Others

Empaths have many unique talents, and being natural diplomats and mediators is one. The ability to tune in to others means you can easily see someone else's side of a situation. This makes empaths great at communicating someone else's perspective to another person or group of people in a clear, compassionate, nuanced way. An empath can read others with opposing views and communicate diplomatically in a way that might better land with others, instead of alienating them.

An empath's naturally strong intuitive system *may* give them information in thoughts, mental downloads, and strong knowings; hearing actual words and sentences in their mind; seeing mental images and pictures in their mind; or having strong feelings, gut instincts, and physical sensations about other people's perspectives (we'll be discussing your intuitive system throughout the book, and how *you personally* receive guidance, in depth later). With all that great intuitive information coming in, it's important to stay in touch with your own perspective.

Anchoring into your own perspective helps you stay true to yourself in business negotiations, family dramas, and decisions both big and small that involve considering the desires of others. In my experience with empath clients, empath friends and family members, and in my own life, empaths can often look back and realize that they didn't argue or defend their point or perspective enough in important situations in their personal and professional lives. They went along with what others wanted because their own wants and needs got lost in the mix—even to themselves. Failing to honor your own perspective is not only harmful to the empath, it robs others of any benefit an empath's perspective would have brought to the situation. Your perspective might have been the healing medicine that a financial, health, or other type of situation required.

Be aware that, as an empath, you need to remind yourself to regularly touch base with your own perspective. That way, you'll feel more satisfied and at peace with any compromises you make with others.

CROWN YOUR INNER SOVEREIGN

STEP 1: Close your eyes and take some deep breaths. Quiet your mind to come home to yourself.

STEP 2: Imagine a beautiful crown, like a king, queen, or monarch would wear in the days of old. It might be covered in rare jewels, or it might be simple and rustic. It could be a crown you saw in a history book or a favorite movie, or a crown in the style your ancestors might have worn or in the style of a culture or time period you feel drawn to.

STEP 3: Now place this imaginary crown on your own head. Feel the gentle weight of it and the power and authority it symbolizes.

STEP 4: Consider a situation with a loved one, coworker, or group of people where you feel torn, confused, or unsure of how to proceed or what is best.

STEP 5: Simply ask yourself what you want and need. If you were a king, queen, or monarch from days of old, and could simply decree something, what would your royal order or command be in this situation? While a good monarch would be compassionate to others and act in the highest good for all, they would also take their own needs and preferences into account. If you were a monarch about to confer with trusted advisers, knowing you had the most power to influence the situation, what would you push for?

STEP 6: Slowly open your eyes and stretch. Considering what's best for others, and what is in the best interest for all, is important, and something you're probably naturally good at. After this meditation, you now hopefully have a better idea of what *you* want and need—that's important too!

> ## MANTRA
> My perspective is important. Others benefit, in ways I may never fully realize, from my honest perspective.

Owning Your Sacred Power

As I sat down to write this section of the book, I was immediately bombarded with memories of times when I did *not* own my sacred power. Past situations with friends, lovers, bosses, and others came back to me as images in my mind's eye—this is *clairvoyance*, the visual intuitive pathway. So if you relate strongly to this section of the book, you are not alone!

Healthy power boundaries in a relationship mean that power should be equal and balanced. So why might empaths *especially* need to maintain clear, healthy boundaries? When your energetic heart can so easily go out to others and feel what they feel, it is more easy to become enmeshed with others. It becomes difficult to distinguish your emotional experience from that of another. Enmeshment could make you more easily pulled along by another's will or emotional experience, or controlled by another's agenda. This might look like becoming very anxious at work because your boss is often very anxious, and then mimicking the way your supervisor approaches their work instead of finding your own relationship to your job. Or it might look like letting your partner take the lead on all the major family decisions because they are very strong-willed.

No matter what your personal spiritual beliefs are, we can all probably agree that each human was born with an inherent amount of power called free will. Some people were born into extremely challenging circumstances where their free will was severely compromised, and others might go through experiences in life where their free will is temporarily restricted. Yet spiritually speaking, humans innately—ideally—are meant to have an enormous amount of free will.

Owning your power is about remembering that in any family, social, or work dynamic, you have power. Exercising that power might look like saying "no" to a social invite, even when you sense that a friend really wants you to say "yes," because you need space and alone time. Or it might look like talking to your manager about a coworker who is chronically late, even if that coworker has a decent excuse each time and part of you sympathizes with them. Or it might look like standing up for social justice or trying to even the power balance in the world so you and others have more fair access to sacred power.

If you don't exercise your personal power in healthy, balanced, compassionate ways, others may not recognize or respect your right to it. Sometimes the only way to get the respect of others is to diplomatically and safely flex your power muscles a little. Remember, your power is sacred.

DISCERN WHEN & WHY YOU GIVE YOUR POWER AWAY

The following exercise is not intended to judge anyone from your past or make anyone wrong. Instead, it will help you to discern instances in the past when you gave your power away, so you can minimize this going forward. Awareness around this issue isn't about doing things in a perfect way, just trying to do things in a healthier way.

If you were victimized by someone in the past, having your power not given away by you but rather stolen from you by someone else, please don't use that painful experience as the focus for this exercise. What we are examining here may be more subtle: times when you allowed or even encouraged others to co-opt your power. This can still be a very victimizing experience and something you should never judge or shame yourself for.

For the following exercise, be gentle with yourself and start small, with relationships and memories that are not too triggering or complex. Start with simple, straightforward situations that could become ideal templates for owning your power in more everyday interactions.

STEP 1: Set aside a few minutes in meditation or with your journal to recall times in the past when you didn't respect your own power, and therefore neither did others. Remember to practice radical self-love. We often only do better when we know better.

STEP 2: Notice what intuitive information you are getting about a past situation. You may see a neighbor's face in your mind, or hear an ex-coworker's name in your mind. You could have thoughts and insights about a past relationship pop into your mind fully formed, or you may think of a company you worked for and get chills or goosebumps.

STEP 3: As you gently sit with these memories, ask yourself if you notice any patterns. Did you feel disempowered by one of your guardians as a child, and has that now become a familiar pattern you fall into as an adult? Do you typically relinquish power in certain situations, like casual, romantic, friendship, family, or professional environments?

STEP 4: Only spend a few minutes on this at a time so you don't overwhelm yourself with memories or emotions. Congratulate yourself for being willing to look at the past—it takes love and courage. Give yourself a hug or tell yourself, "I love you" or "I'm proud of you."

If this—or any exercise in the book—brings up memories or emotions that feel overwhelming, reach out to a supportive loved one or counselor. There can be a lot to untangle from our past wounds, conditioning, and habits. Healing old patterns takes time—be very kind to yourself! Self-love is always the right medicine in any situation.

> **MANTRA**
> Owning my sacred power is how I show myself respect,
> and also how I might elicit more respect from others.

Standing Your Ground

Empaths who own their sacred power and can come home to their own perspective, or know where they stand on an issue, might still struggle with standing their ground. That's because standing your ground—or consistently sticking to or voicing what you think is best—involves being exposed for longer periods to the uncomfortable, challenging emotions of others who have contradictory views or agendas.

In my experience, empaths need to get used to standing their ground, building up the courage and tools to do so. While being an empath affords you many natural talents, the ability to stand your ground *may* not come naturally to you. Yet each empath is wonderfully unique, so your personality and life history/circumstances will greatly factor in.

An ideal example of standing your ground might be having to enforce a healthy habit with your child, like limiting their screen time, and constantly having your child push back on this. Or perhaps you have to implement a healthy budget, green-living practice, or safety protocol at your workplace and continually get pushback from other employees. How does a sensitive empath handle a sustained assault on their emotional and energetic balance?

Practicing how to observe and witness people instead of feeling with them is key, and something we will be working on throughout the book. It's also helpful to stay in touch with your "why," or why you feel this issue is so important to your overall well-being or the overall well-being of others. Empaths feel deeply and can care deeply, so your "why" is powerful. These two methods—witnessing others and connecting with your "why"—should help mitigate what is, unfortunately, an uncomfortable situation for empaths. But if the issue is important to you, it's worth standing your ground.

Keep in mind that there may be relationships in your life where it's comfortable to stand your ground, and other relationships where it's more challenging. You may, in time, build up a healthy callus around sitting with pushback from others, so standing your ground becomes more natural and easier. Then, as others get used to your being able to stand your ground, they may be more accepting of your positions and decisions.

ROOT WITH TREE ENERGY

STEP 1: Find a tree you can connect with. It could be a willow in your back yard, a palm tree on a beach boardwalk, a famous tree you find a picture of online like the Angel Oak, or a tree you find a picture of in a famous forest like a California redwood or a Colorado aspen.

STEP 2: Spend some time tuning in to this tree's energy—empaths have a unique ability to do this! You could sit beneath it, run your hand along its bark, or meditate with an image of that tree in your mind. If the tree is in a park or other public place that you can visit, be sure you do so safely, when other people are around, and in the daytime.

STEP 3: The next occasion you have to stand your ground at home, at work, or in the world, imagine yourself as that tree. You have a protective bark that can deflect anything unwanted, like other people's challenging emotions, and you also have strong, deep roots that reach far into the earth and help you stand tall and sturdy despite the occasional emotional storm or wind gust.

STEP 4: Get clear on your "why." Exactly why are you standing your ground on this issue? Make it an easy sentence or two that gets right to the point, so you can remember your "why" during challenges. You might even write your "why" down in your journal or on a sticky note. When your thoughts focus on the challenging feelings of others, gently take your mind back to your "why."

> **MANTRA**
> I'm getting better at standing my ground on important issues for as long as it benefits me and others to do so.

Understanding the Art of Compromise

Empaths can be masters at the art of compromise! Your ability to intuitively feel into all the layers of someone else's opinions and desires, and even how far they may be willing to compromise, makes negotiating skills something you may become valued or known for in your family or professional life.

Empaths can not only sense what someone wants, but how *badly* they want it. This might even lead you to stay in a relationship—like a romance or a work role—simply because you can feel how upset others would be if you left. In exiting a romance, you might tune in to not only the potential disappointment and pain of the person you are dating or partnered with, but that of their extended family and friends. In a team setting at work, you might sense the frustration a group of people would feel at your departure.

Yet you are not responsible for other people's feelings, or their lives. Trust that, as you get your own needs met, others will find ways to get their needs met as well. Surrender to a power greater than yourself and let that take over the details so you don't get caught trying to control everything for everyone. If you fear that a decision you make will cause someone else to spiral out of control, or put your safety at risk, consult a counselor, health-care professional, law enforcement representative, advocate, or legal expert for advice.

In general, while you may feel someone's challenging emotions in your own system today, their emotions will change and evolve over time. Protecting others from their own challenging emotions *in the moment* by giving too much in a compromise might be protecting that person from their own healthy evolution and transformation.

Compassionate empaths can honor their sensitivity to others by being as kind as possible when compromising. This might look like giving a longer-than-normal notice when leaving a job—if that works for you— or offering to help train or leave instructions for the new person. Or it might look like recommending a counselor or massage therapist to your partner—or having money for such services set aside—to help them cope during your separation and divorce.

Empaths can sometimes make decisions merely to calm the immediate emotions and energies around them. Instead, when compromising, use your powerful intuition to imagine how you will feel in different scenarios *later*. This is activating your *clairsentient* or "feeling" psychic pathway, something all empaths are naturally strong in. Can you sense feelings of bitterness, regret, or longing in your system when you imagine yourself after a certain compromise that's currently on the table? Or do you imagine yourself feeling relieved, happy, peaceful, or accepting after this compromise?

RECEIVE COMMUNICATION ASSISTANCE
WITH ARCHANGEL GABRIEL

Angels are benevolent, nondenominational spiritual beings who enjoy helping humans navigate their earthly journeys. Archangels in particular are very powerful, and can be called upon any time by anyone, anywhere. Each archangel has specific skills, and Archangel Gabriel is a master at communication. If the concept of angels does not resonate with you, simply try the following exercise, imagining that you are asking your wise higher self, or your soul, for assistance.

STEP 1: Find a time and place when you can be alone in a quiet spot.

STEP 2: Connect with Archangel Gabriel, or your own wise higher self. Simply close your eyes and set this intention silently in your thoughts—and relax. Notice if the energy changes around you—like it feels heavier, lighter, thicker, or more palpable and alive. Your clairsentient intuitive pathway helps you feel this, so trust it. Angels exist in the energetic realm; and as someone who is sensitive to energy, you may be able to sense their presence.

STEP 3: Now think of the situation where you're compromising. Silently ask Archangel Gabriel or your soul which of these potential compromise options is in your best interests, as well as in the best interests of all involved. Register any words you hear, insightful thoughts you have, images you see, or gut instincts you experience. You might think of each option separately, and notice what physical sensations you get from your intuition with each.

STEP 4: Next, if you have a few options, picture yourself in the future, after each option, and tune in to how you might feel.

STEP 5: To close the exercise, simply thank Archangel Gabriel or your own higher self for this assistance and open your eyes. Archangel Gabriel can also be with you when you're communicating with others, to help you communicate clearly and help others be open to hearing you. You can also set the intention to be more in touch with your soul or higher self before and during an interaction.

> ## MANTRA
> I value myself, my needs, and my desires when compromising, as well as the needs and desires of others, so I can be more at peace with the outcome later.

Nurturing Your Throat Chakra

Chakras are energy centers located throughout your body, like the one at your throat. When your throat chakra is healthy and open, you feel comfortable and safe expressing your thoughts and feelings. I first found out about chakras in my mid-twenties from a psychic in Paris who told me, "All your chakras are very healthy, except your throat chakra, which is ninety percent closed." My friend (who was there with me) and I gasped dramatically when we heard this information, though honestly I had no clue what that meant at the time.

Many of my major traumas happened between the ages of fourteen and nineteen, including my mother being diagnosed with AIDS, my stepfather kicking me out of the house, starting school in a new state where I knew no one, developing a severe eating disorder, my mother dying, being asked to leave a string of other houses, working thirty-five hours a week while still in high school, and failing my final semester of high school. I was threatened with fists and firearms, and I found myself on my own looking for an apartment and full-time job at eighteen, trying to support myself emotionally and financially.

I've had amazing blessings in my life beyond my wildest dreams! And some of my early relationships were wonderfully nurturing. Yet some of my early-relationship stories with others involved abuse, addiction, neglect, and abandonment. One of the unhealthy coping skills I developed back then was not processing my emotions, or even allowing myself to have emotional reactions. A perfect example of this was the day my mom died, on Halloween. I was living in another state, and my mother and I were estranged at the time. My father knocked on my bedroom door that morning, where I sat on my bed dressed in my costume. He told me that my mother had passed in the early hours. I went to high school anyway that day, arriving on time and attending all my classes normally, wearing a face-paint mask that was deeply symbolic. The one healthy way I did process and express my emotions back then was through music, and some days it was my favorite band or album that got me through.

You've probably gone through similar traumatic times in your own life, when it's just all too much and the emotions get put on hold or buried—they certainly do not go away. Emotions can be really overwhelming. For an empath who is so sensitive to the emotions of others, you might want a break by just bypassing your own. A better option is giving yourself time and space to process and express them gradually and regularly so they are less overwhelming and don't build up.

You can express your emotions by writing about your emotions, talking to a safe and supportive person about your emotions, dancing your emotions, channeling your emotions into a creative project, or even singing your emotions. Your ability to express your emotions has a direct effect on your ability to be assertive and advocate for yourself. So, however you process your emotions, remember that being able to do so is a very valuable coping skill that not only facilitates healing; it has a healing ripple effect throughout your life.

HEAL THROUGH SONG

STEP 1: Find a song, album, or playlist that matches your mood. It might be triumphant hip-hop if you are celebrating a big win, or angsty singer/songwriter if you are feeling frustrated or disappointed. If you're missing home and grew up on a farm or in a rural area, you might play your favorite country artist to feel comforted. If you're living in a different country than where you grew up, play music from your homeland.

STEP 2: Listen to your mood music, and sing along, dance along, or just vibe along. Let it take you deeper into yourself and your emotions. This is sacred time when, as an empath, you can tune in to yourself instead of tuning in to others.

STEP 3: If you get tired of this vibe or feel overwhelmed, transition to music that has a neutral energy signature for you. Celtic music, for example, with Gaelic lyrics, helps me feel light and calm.

> ### MANTRA
> Being in touch with my emotions and expressing them regularly makes being assertive and advocating for myself more comfortable and natural.

Recognizing Yourself on the Introvert/ Extrovert Spectrum

When you feel depleted, are you more restored and nourished by your own energy, or by engaging with the energy of others? This is one of the differences between being an introvert or an extrovert. Don't think of the answer as an absolute, but as more of a general inclination. Do think of this as a spectrum, so you might be an empath who is more introverted, more extroverted, or perhaps you land somewhere in the middle.

All empaths need regular quiet time, downtime, or what I call *retreat* time in a low-stimulation setting, so their sensitive systems can rebalance and recover after picking up on so much around them. Just how much retreat time you need might depend, at least partly, on where you fall on the introvert/extrovert spectrum. People who are introverted will generally like more alone time or more time when people around them are all engaged in quieter activities.

In the book *Quiet: The Power of Introverts in a World That Can't Stop Talking*, author and researcher Susan Cain wrote about extroverts sometimes dominating professional meetings and personal conversations because they may be more comfortable with speaking up. People who are more extroverted—who love being in community with others, seek out lots of social interaction, and enjoy collaborating—might naturally feel more at ease in group settings and therefore have an easier time being assertive.

If you identify as more introverted, or if you are just going through a phase where pulling back into your own energy feels more nurturing—like being energized by a walk on your own in a safe area, getting recharged by working on a creative project solo, or finding contentment snuggling up with a great book—look for tools that help you feel more comfortable speaking up in front of others. This could include taking a class or joining a group focusing on public speaking, employing mindfulness techniques that help you minimize or manage social anxiety, or working with an empath talisman.

WORK WITH AN EMPATH TALISMAN

STEP 1: Find a small object you love the feel and look of, which can fit in the palm of your hand or discreetly in your pocket. It might be a small crystal, a heart-shaped stone, a coin or medallion, or a tiny charm like a spirit animal figurine. Empaths can tune in to the energy not only of other people, but also physical objects. Choose an object that makes you feel pleasant, grounded, and calm when you look at it and hold it.

STEP 2: Set the intention that this object will be an anchoring connection to a benevolent spiritual force greater than you, yet part of you and part of everything. You might language this as God or the Goddess, or the energy of nature or collective human compassion. Tell yourself that when you hold this empath talisman, you are not alone, but rather connected to that loving, mighty force and have greater access to grounding empowerment.

STEP 3: The next time you have to be more assertive, hold your empath talisman in your hand or put it in your pocket when communicating to a boss, a creditor, a loved one, or a doctor, for example. Remember that extroverts, and people who fall somewhere in between introvert and extrovert (like me), still need extra help being assertive sometimes! Assertiveness can be the gateway to getting more of what you want and need in life, so it's a skill worth honing.

> ### MANTRA
> When life asks me to be assertive, I have tools to help myself feel more comfortable communicating with others.

Balancing Energy Exchanges

Energy isn't necessarily something you can see, but something that empaths can easily sense and feel in themselves, in others, in physical spaces, in nature, and in physical objects. Whenever two people, or a group of people, interact, whether it's on the phone, over social media, or in person, there is an energy exchange. Because empaths are so sensitive to energy, they can easily tell when the energy exchange between themselves and others feels off. This is valuable information to have, as someone who is less sensitive might take longer to register that a certain person makes them feel anxious, drained, uncomfortable, or simply off.

When I do a one-on-one session with a client, there is an enormous exchange of energy. However, for me, this feels balanced. That's because I get paid enough money from clients that I can pay my own bills; my clients respect my time and are kind, considerate, lovely people; and I don't think too much about clients before our session/premeditation time starts or after our session ends. Those are great energy boundaries for me. The client, in return, gets 110 percent of me when we're in a session—my complete intuitive focus and my most compassionate self—so I hope they feel it's a balanced exchange for them as well.

If an energy exchange is not balanced, it serves neither person. Therefore, having good energy boundaries for yourself is actually a service to others. If you feel like the energy is off between you and someone else—they are always asking something of you, they seem to talk only about themselves (and you're not their coach, intuitive, or counselor), you dread seeing their name appear on your phone or in your inbox—try adjusting the energy boundaries. Many times this can be done successfully.

You'll know it's a more even or balanced energy exchange when you look forward to hearing from this person, your energy feels light or calm around them, or you simply have a neutral emotional reaction to them. If you find yourself having lots of resentful thoughts about someone, or you are always worried about pleasing them, this is *not* an even and healthy energy exchange.

One easy way to try rebalancing your energy with someone else is to pull back and give yourself more space from them. You might have experienced someone trying this with you, where for a while you just didn't hear from them as much. Try not to take this personally. The other person may just need space in general to rebalance their own energy. If they need a little space from you, fill that extra space in your life with self-love. Then do some loving self-reflection and see if maybe you need to show up to this relationship in a healthier, more balanced way.

You don't have to ghost someone to create space. You can create space from someone in a loving and compassionate way by telling them you're super-busy with family or work, telling them you are tired and resting, or simply staying in touch with them regularly but for much shorter amounts of time—like having shorter phone calls or just texting instead of phoning. Play with and get creative about compassionately creating space from someone. If these techniques don't work, and if you feel threatened or scared in any way, pull back as necessary to protect yourself and contact someone who can help. I've been in that situation myself, and one of the smartest things I did was reach out for help.

While relationships can go through phases where the energy balance feels off temporarily, in general try to keep things balanced as best you can. And, as an empath, get the space you require to stay in balance with yourself.

FEEL THE ENERGY IN YOUR PALM CHAKRAS

STEP 1: Hold your hands open and look at your palms. There is a chakra or energy center located in each. You might imagine a beautiful flower opening in each of your palms, or imagine a color—like purple, pink, green, or yellow—radiating from them.

STEP 2: Now place your hands side by side, palms open and facing each other, about four inches apart. Gently focus your mind on the powerful energy chakras there. Hold your hands this way for a few minutes and let the energy build up in the open space between your palms.

STEP 3: Notice what you felt from your energy body—did your palms tingle or heat up? Was there a heavy, electric, or palpable energy emanating from your palms? I learned about palm chakras from an energy healer who let the energy build up between his palms, and then asked me to place my hand in the open space between them. When I did, I was amazed at what I felt—his energy body had created such a strong, thick current that it was difficult and uncomfortable for me to hold my hand there or move my hand. You might try that exercise with an energy-sensitive friend and see what they feel!

> ### MANTRA
> My energy body extends farther out from my physical body because it's larger than my physical body. My energy body sends me valuable information about people and relationships in my life.

Practicing Radical Receiving

Since empaths can easily sense what others need, they can tend to overgive. This is a theme we will explore throughout the book. Mindfully practicing receiving, and getting more accustomed to receiving, can actually encourage you to be more assertive about asking for what you want and need.

You can set the intention to be more open to receiving—or more mindfully align with receptive energy—at any time. Consciously choosing the energy you want to align with is one way that empaths—who are naturally sensitive to energy—can utilize their sensitivity to more proactively cocreate their lives or positively influence how other people show up in relationship to them.

RECEIVE RADICALLY FOR ONE WEEK

STEP 1: Pick a week on the calendar that will be ideal for receiving. A week with a ton of deadlines at work, or when loved ones are coming for the holidays, may not be best. Start the exercise the afternoon or night before the week begins, like Saturday if your radical receiving week will begin on a Sunday.

STEP 2: Mindfully set the intention to let others give to you for one week. Do this by saying a prayer silently, creating a ritual, setting the intention on a mindful walk or during meditation, or writing your intention down in your journal or somewhere you can see it, like on your bathroom mirror or the fridge.

STEP 3: The day after you set your intention, wake up open to receiving! Watch for any resistance you have to receiving. If someone offers to give to you, and you feel yourself starting to decline their offer, stretch yourself to allow receiving. Because you've set an intention, and it's on your radar to be open to receiving, you may find that life sends you more opportunities to receive.

STEP 4: Play with receptive energy—like trying to be more relaxed and peaceful, or moving through your day more slowly and less aggressively. Remember how your energy felt whenever you were pampered in the past! As you attune your energy to receiving, see if the energy around you responds in kind.

STEP 5: Keep this up for the next seven-day cycle. You can tell others about your experiment (this could be fun if you have small kids and want to encourage them to practice giving), or keep it your little secret between yourself and the universe. If you forget your experiment at any point, just gently get back on track. You can also receive radically by pampering yourself in a way that's healthy but also indulgent!

Communicating with Compassionate Honesty

Being able to feel in your own system what others are feeling can make some empaths very compassionate and tenderhearted, or nervous about upsetting someone or hurting another person's feelings. I call these folks earth angels, and I wrote a whole book about them called *Are You an Earth Angel?* If this describes you, know that being very compassionate and tenderhearted is a lovely quality worth celebrating in yourself. Every character trait, however, has its wonderful aspects, and also its more challenging aspects.

You might have a friend—whether they are an empath or not—who *isn't* so tenderhearted. While this friend might be very blunt, you at least know you are always getting their honest opinion, which is valuable. You might advise your friend to "put a little sugar on it" before they speak. Yet your blunt friend might advise *you* to "just tell it to me straight," or be more honest in your communication.

Tenderhearted empaths should remember that sometimes telling someone else your honest opinion is a real kindness, and that it can be done in a compassionate way, so you still honor that sweet side of yourself. You might even start to become known for your communication style—sweet and straight up!

If you're an empath who is nervous about upsetting others, or you are having trouble feeling compassion toward the person you want to communicate compassionately with, the following exercise should help!

CONNECT WITH YOUR HEART CHAKRA
BEFORE COMMUNICATING

STEP 1: To connect with your energetic heart or heart chakra, simply put your hand over your physical heart. Take a few deep breaths, close your eyes, and notice if you can sense a soft, tender energy enveloping you. It might also help to imagine anything that usually makes you feel soft and tender, like picturing a child in your life or a favorite pet, or the face of a character in a favorite show who learns the power of forgiveness.

STEP 2: The next time you need to communicate honestly and compassionately with someone, take a few minutes to connect with your heart chakra first. While doing this, send some love to yourself.

STEP 3: Plan out what you want to say ahead of time, and try to be as direct as possible. Remind yourself of reasons why honesty from you might benefit this person, like helping them see their blind spots, not enabling their poor behavior, or improving their relationship and intimacy level with you by knowing how you really feel.

STEP 4: After you communicate with this person, pause again to connect with your heart chakra and send yourself some love.

If it's too hard to connect to compassion because you are really angry, disappointed, frustrated, anxious, or triggered, see if you can put off the conversation temporarily until you feel more neutral and have had time to do more processing of your emotions as well as getting more support.

You can also call on any higher power—like the communication guru Archangel Gabriel we already worked with in this chapter—for assistance. Archangel Chamuel is the angel of peace, and calling on that spirit helper can actually make empaths who are particularly energy sensitive feel calmer.

Activating Witnessing/Observer Mode During Confrontations

Most humans tend to shy away from confrontation, but for sensitive empaths confrontation comes with extra challenges. Empaths naturally fear upsetting others, because empaths can feel the challenging emotions of other people in their own system. So if you have to confront your teen about a bad habit they have fallen into, and your teen is going through an intensely rebellious phase, as an unprepared empath you could feel very intense yourself after confronting your teen and have trouble settling your sensitive system down for hours, maybe even days. Or worse, you might avoid confrontation altogether.

Empaths have two modes they can choose in any situation: opening up to feel with someone, or pulling back into their own energy to witness and observe others. It can be a mindful choice, or your system can automatically kick into either mode as well. Empaths' default or natural response can be opening up to feel.

When sitting with a grieving friend, your empath heart might naturally open to grieve and cry with them, which, if you have the emotional reserves, can be a very nourishing experience for both you and your friend. If you're feeling drained going into the same situation, you can mindfully choose the witnessing/observer mode. You are still sitting with your friend and comforting them by patting their back or whispering soothing words, but you are not feeling with them.

Remember that observing and witnessing does not make you cold, uncaring, or remote. Sometimes holding a calm, compassionate, grounded space for someone is more supportive than feeling with them, whether what they are feeling is intensely pleasant or intensely painful. I'm very good at observing and witnessing, which allows me to work as an intuitive so intimately in one-on-one sessions with clients. I believe my childhood and teen years played a role, when witnessing and observing became part of the way I dealt with trauma and the intense emotions of adults around me, starting with my parents' divorce when I was four. Now as an adult, I use witnessing and observing not so much as an unconscious trauma response, but consciously as a way to support myself and others. As a compassionate empath, you'll have a much larger bandwidth for supporting loved ones, clients, coworkers, and the world in general when you can show up in witnessing/observer mode.

Practice witnessing/observer mode by:

- **Imagining space between your energy body and someone else's,** as if you are holding their energy and emotions at arm's length..
- **Going into your head about their emotions instead of your heart.** You can do this by getting curious about what they are experiencing or feeling, or naming it.
- **Activating your claircognizance or intellectual psychic pathway** to help turn the volume down on your clairsentience or feeling psychic pathway. Pay attention to ah-ha realizations, breakthrough thoughts, and intuitive downloads.

You'll know you are in witnessing/observer mode when your own emotions and energy remain neutral—as opposed to intense, or very high or very low—even while people around you are experiencing more extreme energy and emotions. It's not a perfect practice, but with time and awareness you will notice the benefits! We'll be working with witnessing/observer mode throughout the book, and we will continue to explore different ways to approach and employ it.

It's okay to be playful about entering witnessing/observer mode! If you have a manager or family member who can be emotionally intense, and you need to confront them about requesting time off from work or about missing a family get-together, you might tell yourself, "Shields up!" Then, just like in science fiction shows, you can imagine yourself as a starship that is employing your shielding defense technology, so that any incoming intense emotions are deflected and bounced back into outer space.

ENTER WITNESSING/OBSERVER MODE
BEFORE A CONFRONTATION

STEP 1: If possible, give yourself a few minutes to prepare before the confrontation. Not too much time, as that could create anticipatory stress, which can be an issue for empaths. Confrontations can happen organically, so there's no preparatory time. With practice you'll be able to enter witnessing/observer mode very quickly. Try to catch the other person when they display a more neutral energy or mood, or are not feeling too intense.

STEP 2: Take a few deep breaths, and put your hand over your heart. Imagine a gentle energy bubble forming around you that is calm and protective. Give it a color or texture if you like. If you want to call on a higher power to be with you during the confrontation, like an angel or guide, or you'd like to grab your empath talisman to hold or slip in your pocket, now is the time. Feel that extra grounding support and strength coming in energetically.

STEP 3: Get clear on what you'll say. Practice in your mind so you're easy to understand, diplomatic, and as brief and to-the-point as possible.

STEP 4: Imagine a couple of ways the other person might react, to reduce your chances of being thrown off by how they respond. As you are able to witness and observe, holding a neutral energy, you might find that the other person *mirrors* your own grounded energy. Humans tend to mirror other people's energy automatically, which is something you can take advantage of in confrontations.

STEP 5: While communicating with the other person—whether face-to-face, on the phone, or over email or text—imagine space between your energy body and theirs. Give them time to process and respond, and try to maintain an open, neutral attitude. Get curious about their reaction and stay in your head. You can go into your heart more later: after the confrontation, when you can be alone; or with a safe and supportive person to do some emotional processing.

If someone is abusive or exhibiting toxic behavior, get extra support from loved ones or a counselor before you proceed with a confrontation. Witnessing/observer mode is never meant to encourage you to tolerate an unhealthy or abusive relationship.

> ### MANTRA
> Confrontations are the perfect time to practice witnessing/observer mode. When I can hold a neutral, grounded energy, others might mirror that back to me.

Not Minimizing Yourself for Others

While some people might inflate themselves in front of others to compensate for their insecurities, an empath might *minimize* their attributes and achievements if they sense that someone else is insecure. This behavior does not serve an empath, for example, when they need to be assertive in their career—minimizing yourself in front of colleagues and clients can limit the amount of recognition or raises you receive. It might also enable narcissistic tendencies in others, so they get used to controlling what is said and not said, or the energy and mood of the room.

Being humble is a good thing. It's also good to sense that others are insecure and not tap-dance all over their wounds. But remember that minimizing yourself in front of others can become a bad habit. Minimizing your accomplishments to others could lead to minimizing other things, like minimizing your emotional experience to others—or even to yourself. You'll know if you've minimized yourself in front of others in an unhealthy way when your own energy feels deflated after the exchange.

Conversely, being gracious and compassionately aware of other people's wounds and insecurities when you speak about yourself to others has a soft, gentle, warm energy. That can make you feel nourished by the conversation, or more intimately connected with someone after the exchange. This could look like sharing, with a friend who is going through a hard time, that you've just reached a huge milestone you'd worked long and hard for in your career or personal life. Then following that up with, "Like everyone, I've had some amazing blessings in my life. It makes the disappointments and the heartbreaks so much easier to bear." Empaths can use their unique sensitivity to honor themselves and others so that everyone is seen and considered in conversation.

BUILD YOURSELF UP

STEP 1: Sit down with a journal and list what you admire most about yourself. This could include: accomplishments, natural talents or character traits, skills you've honed, healthy risks you've taken, stuff you are only beginning to accomplish or work toward, times you've shown up for loved ones, people you've helped, big obstacles you've overcome, or tiny ways you try to be a kind person each day.

STEP 2: Next, ask caring, supportive loved ones and colleagues to share what they most admire about you. If you feel self-conscious about asking, you can always tell them it's an exercise in a book! (Be sure to return the favor and do the same for them.) Also think back to some of the best compliments you have ever received—these often stick out in our memories. Make a list of what others admire about you in your journal.

STEP 3: Keep this list, and refer to it anytime you need a confidence or self-esteem boost!

> ## MANTRA
> We are each admirable in so many ways. Celebrating what's admirable about me and what's admirable in others is a way to lift up, heal, and inspire humanity.

Identifying Your Authentic Yes and Authentic No

Since empaths have an ability to easily see things from other people's perspectives, they might find it easier to be more open-minded, which can make empaths more open to the priorities of others. This is a lovely trait! Where empaths may get into difficulty is that they can so easily focus on others that they lose track of their own priorities.

You might have agreed to something a friend or family member wanted and prioritized, like an expensive vacation during your busy time of year professionally. Then midway through the trip, you find yourself distracted by work emails and obligations, and worrying about your dwindling bank account. If you'd checked in with yourself to decide if this trip was an authentic yes or no for you beforehand, and put your loved one's priorities to the side for a moment, your loved one might have been open to taking the trip at a different time and to a much more affordable locale. You've realized, a little late, that saving money and working on your career are two of your top priorities or yesses right now. While spending time with loved ones and having fun are also important, you could have accomplished that in a more authentic way.

Empaths can get carried along with the tide of other people's wants and needs. Remember, it's better to surf them on the board of your own priorities. Stay centered there so you don't wipe out. Empaths should always ask themselves, How can I make this situation serve me, or more pleasurable for me? It's a wonderful way to anchor into your own energy and prioritize yourself!

LIST YOUR NORTH STAR PRIORITIES

STEP 1: Sit down with your journal and write five, ten, or even fifteen top priorities for you right now. This might include stuff like concentrating on financial health or physical health; achieving in your career or developing your creativity; studying something new or meeting new people; practicing mindfulness and lowering your stress levels; being adventurous or taking healthy risks; or pulling back to nurture yourself or nurturing your close relationships. Anything can be on this list, and items that seem small—like making time and space to connect with yourself each day—might actually be huge. This list is your North Star, or what sailors used to navigate with when lost at sea. You can navigate your relationships with this list whenever you are lost on the sea of others' priorities.

STEP 2: Periodically update this list or create a new one, as our priorities and lives can change so much over the weeks and months. Mentally consult this list any time you receive an invitation from a loved one or a business offer from a colleague, or take your top five priorities and post them where you'll see them regularly. Keep track of older versions of your North Star priorities and see what has changed, evolved, or stayed consistent in your life.

> **MANTRA**
> Knowing my top priorities is key to getting my needs and wants met, and navigating this voyage called life.

HOW ASSERTIVE ARE YOU?

The quizzes in this book are meant to be fun, informative, and thought-provoking. There are no right or wrong answers, and no pass or fail marks. Answer the following questions as honestly as you can, keeping track of your answers, and then check the key at the end.

1. Something seems off about the way a company you partnered with is promoting your product/creation. You:

   a. Get in touch with your contact there, or someone higher up, ASAP. If they don't get back to you immediately, you're annoyed.

   b. Take some time to think through your reservations, formulate a diplomatic and straightforward email, and then share your concerns.

   c. You probably would not say anything. You don't want to look foolish, and you partnered with this company because you didn't want to handle this side of the business.

2. Your in-laws are coming to town and really want to visit a popular tourist spot that you think is super overrated. You:

   a. Tell them it's a waste of time, and forward them some negative online reviews of the destination.

   b. Wait until they arrive at your house, and then let them know there are a few things on their itinerary you're not interested in, so you may skip those, depending on how you feel.

c. Ask your partner what to do. After all, these are not your parents, and you want to avoid being the heavy.

3. A good friend's number pops up on your phone. You know he wants to talk again about ongoing issues he's having at work, but you've had a crazy day yourself and need to veg. You:

a. Pick up quickly and tell him you can't talk. There was a lot of noise in the background since you were walking to the subway, and you were harried so the conversation was brief, but at least you responded.
b. Let it go to voicemail. After you've eaten dinner and settled in for the evening, you'll text him and explain that it's a bad night to chat but that you'll call tomorrow.
c. Sigh, groan, and pick up after a few rings. You adopt a welcoming tone and let him unpack his day while you daydream about the movie or book or exercise routine you wish you were unwinding with instead.

4. The specialist doctor you were referred to recommends a new treatment plan, but the consultation went quickly and you have lingering questions about some of the recommended supplements or medications. You:

a. Call the office and ask to be scheduled for an immediate follow-up consult with the doctor, even though it normally takes weeks to get in. It's your health, so you're not taking "no" for an answer.

b. Call the office and speak to the nurse practitioner. This person is able to answer all your big questions. You then ask to be transferred to the receptionist and booked in for the next opening in three weeks.

c. Get anxious, and then talk yourself out of your emotion, and then get anxious again. This cycle continues for days until you decide to do nothing—waiting to start treatment until you can get in to speak to the doctor at your next scheduled appointment.

5. You splurge on a jacket you have been eyeing at your favorite online boutique. The following month you're browsing the same site, and notice the same jacket is now on deep discount. You're familiar with the site's policy, and that the window of time has passed for you to call and receive a credit for the sale price. You:

a. Call anyway, and pretend you don't know the site's policy about adjusting the price, demanding a credit for the difference. You're super bummed and getting worked up while on hold, before even talking to the rep.

b. Feel disappointed for twenty-four hours. The next day you decide it can't hurt to call and ask if the site will make an exception for you, even though you are well past the cut-off time to receive an adjustment for the sale price. You're a regular customer, and being extra polite to the customer service rep might help.

c. Kick yourself for not getting the sale price, although how could you have known? You can't be lucky all the time.

ANSWERED MOSTLY A'S: An Empath Who Isn't Afraid to Put Their Agenda Forward

You have no problem going after what you want directly and speaking your mind! That's a good thing. People who are passive-aggressive, or who hint at what they want in a roundabout way, might drive you nuts. And it might be hard for you to relate to folks who are plain-old passive and have trouble being proactive about their lives. You might consider cultivating assertiveness, or moving confidently and self-assuredly through the world while not being aggressive. At times you could come off to others as pushy, so working on your timing and delivery may get you more of what you want more easily—and make the process less stressful for you.

ANSWERED MOSTLY B'S: An Empath Who Has Mastered the Art of Assertiveness

It's not a perfect practice, but generally you're good at putting yourself forward in a way that's not off-putting to others. You might consider yourself an ambassador to the art of assertiveness, and gently yet powerfully model proactive, respectful communication and behavior to others.

ANSWERED MOSTLY C'S: An Empath Who Might Miss Out by Being Passive

Being assertive can be really uncomfortable for empaths initially, so it's very understandable that after answering the quiz questions honestly, you found yourself in this category. Remember that you are important, and your views, wants, and needs are worthy of sharing and going after. It may not be only you who benefits, but others as well! There are tons of tools in this book to help you get used to and feel more comfortable taking greater ownership of your life and being more assertive.

Chapter 2

Protecting Your Empath Heart

Being an empath is *awesome*. My sensitivity and remarkably high intuitive ability are some of my most treasured character traits. Using the four psychic clairs or pathways—hearing, seeing, knowing, and feeling intuitive guidance—in sessions with clients all over the world is how I earn my living. It provides the nourishing food on my table, as well as the table itself! My sensitivity allows me to connect intimately with strangers who become clients, and helps clients access more information about themselves and their lives so they can better understand, pivot, transform, or heal. These sessions are very precious for both myself and the client, and have been the most phenomenal and connecting experiences of my life.

My energetic empath heart goes out to others and the world at large and helps me relate to people—their experiences and emotions—and feel *with* them so I have more compassion. I can even feel with, and bond with, fictional characters in a book or real people from history—my sensitivity brings them alive for me! Traveling through life as an empath is an incredibly layered, deep experience, one that I would not trade for anything.

You may encounter people positioning the empath experience as one of victimhood. There's plenty of information out there, or plenty of conversations you could join, about how tough it is to be an empath. You can also be told, or have it implied, that your sensitivity makes you somehow "better" than others, or unique, as if you were meant to perch on an empath pedestal above the horde of humanity. I bristle at all this. Yes, there are certain challenges to being an empath, as there are challenges with anything. And yes, your sensitivity makes you *different* from someone who is less sensitive; but you are not therefore inherently kinder, more sparkly, or more worth celebrating. We're *all* sparkly and worth celebrating! And I believe each and every one of us is, inherently, equal and special.

Protecting your empath heart is not about being a martyr to your sensitivity, though surely being sensitive sets you up to possibly experience specific wounds. Protecting your empath heart is about creating empath-specific boundaries in your relationships with others and the world so that you can enjoy and flourish in your sensitivity! There's nothing to fear in this chapter; nothing to brace yourself for. Instead, open to the wisdom here and get curious about the paradoxical notion of protecting your empath heart so that you can experience and share even more of its wondrous, magical gifts.

If being an empath hasn't traditionally been an awesome experience for you, I'm truly sorry. I get it, and I see you. Your personal experience with your sensitivity is valid and real, always. Don't let anyone talk you out of your own emotions and experience. I'm hoping the information in this chapter will help you enjoy your sensitivity more and make you feel more empowered! You deserve that.

Recognizing Signs of Overwhelm and Overstimulation

Have you ever been to an all-day outdoor concert, a weekend workshop, or another big event with a lot going on, and the person you went with seemed unfazed by all the energy and emotion and physical stimuli bouncing around? While you and the friend or colleague you attended the event with both had a great time, afterward you might want to go back to your hotel room for a quiet chill night, do an exercise routine solo, or simply take the next weekend "off" so that you're puttering around the house with no commitments. Your friend or colleague might, however, jump right back into the fray with busy work and social engagements right away . . . while that would frazzle your sensitive system.

Empaths are hyperperceptive, meaning their nervous and energetic systems pick up on more—the energy of a room, the collective emotions of a group—and empaths can actually feel these energies and emotions in their own system. Some empaths are even more sensitive to physical stimuli, so the continuous background chatter of a hotel ballroom where a conference is being held, or the fun loud music pumping in a concert hall, can eventually be overwhelming. Because empaths pick up on more, they are more easily overstimulated and need to have regular downtime in low-stimulation settings to rebalance.

Keep in mind that the amount of downtime, or what I call retreat-and-recover time (we'll explore empath retreat-and-recover activities in the next section), that you require can be different from individual to individual. You also might find that at certain times in your life, or on certain days, you have a higher or lower threshold for stimulation. That's why recognizing the possible signs or symptoms of overstimulation can be so helpful.

Your sensitive system can truly become overstimulated—just like when a computer freezes or crashes because it's unable to process the amount of data coming in. Sensitive people can even get stuck in a cycle of being chronically overstimulated. Not feeling guilty about needing to peace out or slow your roll, and helping family and friends understand that you require this, is a big component to creating nurturing relationships as a sensitive person. As others are willing to make accommodations for your sensitivity, be sure to make loving accommodations for them too—like being mindful of their emotional triggers, their food sensitivities, or anything else they have special requirements around.

RATE YOUR TOP SIGNS OF SENSITIVITY OVERWHELM/ OVERSTIMULATION

STEP 1: Over the coming month, notice when you experience an uptick of any of the following: racing thoughts; feeling physically drained or more tired than usual; feeling physically jumpy, fidgety, tense, or on edge; speeding up and rushing around for no reason; desperately craving alone time; isolating or numbing out in unhealthy ways or increase in addictive behavior; overindulging in junk food like very fatty and salty carbs or sweets, or forgetting to eat altogether; trouble concentrating; becoming reactive, irritable, and cranky for no obvious reason; craving quiet or soft, calm music or being unnerved by loud noises; bingeing television or surfing the Internet for much longer periods of time than you feel is healthy; drinking alcohol more heavily than usual; avoiding responsibilities/chores that normally don't stress you out because these routine activities—like paying bills, cleaning the house, or getting your hair cut—are suddenly "too much"; avoiding important conversations or changes, or extreme procrastination in any area of your life; getting really annoyed by having to participate in work meetings or planned social gatherings; increase in free-floating anxiety, worry, OCD, anticipatory stress, or becoming fixated; trouble falling asleep, waking up in the night repeatedly, or having bad dreams; having trouble letting go of others' energy and emotions—people you know or stories in the news—or increase in social anxiety; or emotional outbursts that are out of character.

STEP 2: When you notice a few or more examples from Step 1 happening in concert, discern if overstimulation of your sensitive system might be the culprit, or part of the issue. Did you have a day, several days, or even several weeks this month when you were not able to get low-stimulation downtime? Stimulation can be cumulative, so work in more retreat-and-recover time to keep your sensitive system in balance. Rate your top five signs of overstimulation—based on the list above or from your own personal experience—so you can recognize when your sensitive system is overwhelmed and course-correct.

STEP 3: Check in with your health-care providers—like doctors, naturopaths, nurse practitioners, therapists, and psychiatrists—to make sure your body and mind are getting all the support they need. Sometimes things like hormone levels, adrenal health, vitamin and mineral levels, diet, brain chemistry, post-traumatic stress, patterns adopted from childhood, circumstantial depression or anxiety, and other issues can play a part. Your life is unique, and so are your personality, history, mind, body, and spirit. Get any support you require!

Having relationships with health-care providers you trust and like is important for empaths. As sensitivity now becomes more widely understood and discussed, you may even find health-care providers who specialize in—or have lots of experience with—sensitive patients/clients. You may also find that as a sensitive person, stimulants and depressants, like coffee and alcohol, have a stronger effect on you.

> ### MANTRA
> There's only so much stimulation my sensitive system can take. I know what being overwhelmed and overstimulated feels like, and it's always a cue to lower the stimulation stakes in my life.

Building In Regular Retreat & Recover Time

What I term "retreat-and-recover" time is, in my opinion, one of the best self-care tools and protection strategies sensitive people have access to.

The concept is incredibly simple—empaths need regular downtime in low-stimulation settings to let their hyperperceptive systems calm and rebalance after being exposed to a lot of emotional, energetic, and physical stimuli.

Retreat-and-recover time could be curling up with a paperback for an hour after a long day at work. Or listening to soft music while cooking a meal with your partner on a sleepy Saturday, when there's no rush or deadline or expectation from anyone. Or it might look like doing a thousand-piece puzzle with your kids, where everyone is quietly considering their next move.

When contemplating how to create a low-stimulation zone for ideal retreat-and-recover time, keep in mind what in your life can be very stimulating:

- **High expectations from yourself or others**, like when you're on a tight deadline at work, trying to get a child to a doctor's appointment on time, or performing for an audience.
- **Activities that require intense focus**, like doing your taxes, figuring out how to put a new piece of furniture together, studying for an exam, or proofreading a report for work.
- **Any environment where there's a lot of physical stimuli**—a popular grocery store at peak hours, a sports event in a packed stadium, a large meeting with continuous background noise, a wedding celebration where you are dancing or hugging a lot.
- **Days when you are juggling many tasks** and responsibilities, or transitioning from one role to the next quickly and often.
- **Being around larger groups of people or new people you don't know as well** and may not feel as comfortable or relaxed around yet. Performing for anyone, like presenting at work or meeting your partner's family.

- **Having a lot on your plate emotionally**—like grieving someone who left your life, or celebrating the birth of a new family member.
- **Having a lot on your plate mentally**—being in a busy season at work, or having lots of deadlines at school.
- **Being the support person for others** at home, at work, or at a volunteer job. Many empaths love to support others and are good at it! But it can also be overwhelming and demand a lot of attention and energy.

Try to establish a rhythm with your life where retreat-and-recover time becomes a regular part of your day, week, and month, almost as if it's a muscle memory for your body. Becoming comfortable with more stimulation is a situation you can get used to, like a mother might get used to the extra stimulation of a second child. Or empaths might be able to develop a healthy emotional and energetic callus to protect against certain stimulation so it fades to the background or can be witnessed and observed instead of being absorbed, like the veteran teacher who can tune out the constant background stimulation of working at a bustling school, or a long-time nurse at a large hospital who can unflinchingly navigate a chaotic emergency room day after day. Having regular retreat-and-recover time might be one of the best ways to increase your overall threshold for stimulation.

Retreat-and-recover time for you might include:

- **Creative hobbies,** like writing, painting, playing a musical instrument, gardening, cooking, jewelry-making, pottery, or knitting.
- **Reading something engaging,** like an interesting biography or memoir, a nonfiction book where you learn something new, or a series of novels you get lost in.
- **Family or group activities that are low stimulation,** like hanging out at the park, going for a nature walk,

puttering around a bookstore or museum, or doing a group crafting activity or baking project.

- **Getting some solo time**, like taking a long bath, listening to a podcast while you tidy or organize a room, taking yourself out to lunch, or taking an online workshop in a subject that fascinates you.

- **Hanging out with someone who you feel really comfortable around** and don't have to perform for, like playing or snuggling with a favorite pet or meeting an old friend for coffee.

- **Cruising your favorite haunts**—like a record store or thoughtfully curated shop—on the off-peak hours when it's a chill environment.

- **Lowering the physical stimulation mindfully,** like dimming the lights in a room, cleaning up any distracting clutter, putting on nature sounds, or spraying mild aromatherapy scents.

- **Making your body physically comfortable,** like snuggling under a weighted blanket, sitting on your most cozy furniture, making a cup of your favorite soothing beverage, or getting the room temperature dialed in just right.

- **Engaging in gentle physical activity,** like taking a slow-moving stretch yoga class or a leisurely stroll around the neighborhood.

- **Letting the body be still**, like getting everything ready to enjoy your favorite movie so you don't have to keep jumping up to grab something.

- **Carving out a bit of time when you can avoid anything overly stressful or dramatic,** like not checking your email for a bit in the afternoon or not reading a disturbing news story right before bed.

IDENTIFY IDEAL RETREAT & RECOVER TIMES & ACTIVITIES

STEP 1: Get curious about when you can work in more retreat-and-recover time. Could you wake up twenty minutes earlier each day to meditate, sit and enjoy your morning pick-me-up beverage on the porch, write in your journal, or pull an oracle card for yourself? Can you take thirty minutes in the middle of the day to walk your neighborhood or a safe park near your office? In the evening, how can you carve out retreat-and-recover time alone as well as with your children, pets, roommates, or partner? What time on the weekends is ideal to set aside for regular retreat-and-recover time?

STEP 2: Identify your favorite retreat-and-recover activities. Remember that you don't have to be alone to have quality retreat-and-recover time. However, empaths usually love their alone time! If this is you, it's something you may have to gently explain to lovers, friends, and older children so they know that it's nothing personal but sometimes you just need space in general. This is why when a social engagement is canceled at the last minute, an empath's first reaction may be relief—even though they really enjoy and value the person they were supposed to hang out with!

> ### MANTRA
> When I need to soothe my sensitive system, I don't have to isolate or numb out with unhealthy coping skills. I have retreat-and-recover activities that are engaging, calming, and always available when I need them.

Using Humor to Shield Yourself and Lighten Energy

Empaths are not only good at sensing energy, they can also create it. I'm a huge fan of humor and playful energy. Have you ever listened to a friend venting about an issue that's frustrating them, and you sensed a point in the conversation where you could make a joke and lighten the energy? Using humor to diffuse a tense situation or create a lighter energy in a group dynamic—like making a joke to connect everyone in laughter during a family reunion when people are getting cranky—is an excellent way to balance energy when it feels very serious or thick. Think of the collective energy of a room full of folks or between just two people as a stew: you can add merely a dash of something—like one short, witty comment and a sly smile—to significantly alter the overall flavor of the energetics.

Being able to discern the collective energy and emotions of a room, a small group of people, or an individual makes empaths able to discern when it's an appropriate moment to make a wisecrack—and when it might be tone-deaf or fall flat. There are occasions when humor is just downright insensitive and uncalled for. Often, though, you can validate another person's emotional experience and witness them lovingly while also finding moments to make them—and you—smile.

Humor, at its best, offers people a break from their worries and puts life into perspective. Simply watching a comedy with a friend or forwarding someone a funny social media post can be a welcome break for them and for you. Humor can be like glue, helping long-term relationships stick together. One could argue that if you can laugh with someone, you can stay in relationship to them.

Everyone has different tastes where humor is concerned. You may have grown up in an environment where teasing was very normal, encouraged, and a sign of affection. However, you might have since learned as an adult that some people really don't enjoy being teased. Others absolutely light up when you tease pretty hard, making a game out of it, teasing and bantering back and forth. Some people prefer to be teased in subtle, very loving ways, and still others may have a no-teasing rule. They might wear a shirt that says, "Tease hair, not people!"

Empaths have a unique ability to sense how others respond to different types of humor. Sometimes energy from others—like how they react to a joke you share—even hits your body or registers very physically for an empath. As you travel through life making new friends, becoming part of new groups and families and work or spiritual communities, play with humor as a way to connect and bond deeply with others, discerning how and when humor is appreciated with different individuals.

Humor can even be a way for empaths to bond quickly with others and feel more comfortable in new environments. New work settings or family dynamics or communities might be a lot for an empath who can intimately feel the natural social awkwardness of other people trying to welcome them.

When I moved to a new state in sixth grade and started middle school, I was a total stranger to a large group of kids from a relatively small town who had grown up together for years. At the time, I lived with a family member who always listened to stand-up comedy, and without consciously realizing it I began to use humor at school to protect myself from the harsher realities of life. Being the new kid, and an empath, made me pick up on all the who-the-heck-is-she energy I was getting from the entire school. Humor helped shield me from the overwhelming vulnerability I felt walking into a new classroom each day recognizing no one. In school I learned to both laugh and make jokes with the kids sitting near me, and use humor to defuse situations with insecure kids. At home I learned to laugh at myself and hone my humor chops in a household that very much valued humor.

A group of "popular" girls, all of whom were considered physically beautiful or came from families who were considered wealthy, who sat together every day in the cafeteria began inviting me to sit with them because I was "so funny." (It certainly wasn't because I was considered physically beautiful, and my single mother was lower middle class and at various times technically below the poverty line.) Eventually I made friends of all types of kids from all different groups in the school: the "smart" kids, the "sporty" kids, the "creative" kids, kids from different ethnic backgrounds, kids from all different financial realities, and the amazing, in some cases very sensitive, kids who had trouble fitting in.

As an empath I could relate to them all, and I used humor to help shield me from the normal awkwardness of getting to know new people. I had my moments of feeling lonely and like an outsider, but humor helped mitigate that. In my yearbook, the most common comment people wrote down was, "You are hilarious!" I learned that all these different kids— who were all unique individuals—each valued humor, and that humor could actually protect me. A compassionate sense of humor can be a considerable ally.

CLAIM YOUR SACRED CLOWNS

STEP 1: Identify people in popular culture or in your own personal life who make you laugh! It might be a coworker who cracks dry, sarcastic comments in conversation; a family member who is a master at physical humor, always making funny faces and silly-dancing around the room; or a professional comedian whose career you follow. Who do you turn to when you need to smile?

STEP 2: Observe how these funny folks use humor to defuse situations, lighten energy, put life into perspective, bond with others and deepen relationships, or shield and protect themselves. Pay particular attention to people who employ humor in combination with heart energy and compassion, using humor in a kind, respectful way.

> ### MANTRA
> Humor is an energy ally that's multi-purpose. I can use it to protect myself, shift the collective energetics, or bond with others.

Acting as a Respected Mediator Instead of a Rescuer or Referee

Are you the person in your family, at your workplace, or in your friend group who gets called in to settle disputes, negotiate terms, or carry a message from one person or department to another? We've already touched upon how empaths can have a natural ability to be successful diplomats, messengers, and negotiators. You may be able to intuitively read a situation, discern what's possible and probable, and tune into how all sides feel about an issue or how much they may be willing to compromise. This can make empaths invaluable when individuals or groups with different views and agendas need to get on the same page. Being able to empathize with various and even opposing perspectives makes you a powerful and compassionate advocate for everyone involved.

You might have also experienced times when helping other people communicate with and understand each other became like a full-time job! When you have the time in your schedule and emotional reserves inside yourself, it can be fun or nourishing to help others find a way through tough impasses, or it could feel fulfilling to engage in an activity your sensitivity might set you up to be naturally blessed at. But mediating between individuals or groups of people is something you must do on *your* terms, not anyone else's.

Empaths may feel *compelled* to act as mediator simply because they don't want to feel all the challenging emotions of others in their own system. So getting everyone calm, satisfied, or in agreement means the empath can sit back and just absorb some good vibes instead of all those conflict vibes! Yet there are much healthier, quicker, easier, kinder, and more productive ways for you to protect your empath heart—you don't have to resort to placating, people-pleasing, emotional manipulation, rescuing, or refereeing. People, being instinctively focused on getting their own needs met, often don't realize when they're draining others and asking too much. You may have to self-impose boundaries so you remain a mediator and don't become a referee or a rescuer.

Refereeing can look like:

- Having to constantly defuse situations or calm people down.
- Breaking up heated arguments and debates.
- Enforcing rules, ethics, or polite social norms people should be following anyway.
- Feeling like people will be at each other's throats or situations will become chaotic if you aren't there to keep order.
- Feeling on edge or on red alert, even anticipating certain individuals or groups of people interacting, like seeing an event in the future on your calendar and being filled with dread.
- Being pulled away from your own life or concerns and feeling distracted, frustrated, or resentful about your role as a mediator.

Bottom line: Unless people want to pay you top dollar, hand you a whistle and a special uniform, and abide by your calls, avoid becoming a referee!

Rescuing can look like:

- Enabling the poor behavior of others because you are always ready to jump in and fix the situation, solve problems, or make everything okay for everyone involved.
- Encouraging people to act like toddlers by not holding them accountable for emotionally immature or inappropriate behavior with others.
- Becoming codependent with others so that they don't feel they can manage conflict without you, and you feel validated that someone needs you so desperately.
- Feeling physically exhausted or emotionally drained by mediating.

Bottom line: Unless you are a lifeguard, EMT, or firefighter, leave rescuing to the professionals.

Being a respected mediator can look like:

- Getting a compliment from loved ones after a family gathering, or getting a compliment on your yearly review at work about your amazing mediator skills!
- Feeling genuine contentment and satisfaction at using one of your gifts to help others.
- An increased sense of healthy self-worth or self-confidence.
- Receiving from others, like having a friend treat you to lunch after you offered her advice on how to mediate with her mother, or having a supervisor give you a raise to reflect your rockstar mediation skills.
- Encouraging others in a productive and compassionate way to improve their own communication skills and emotional intelligence.

Bottom line: Any activity you engage in often will create a built-up energy around you that others might unknowingly pick up on. The more you act as a respected mediator, the less people may come to you looking for a rescuer or referee.

REVISIT YOUR HISTORY AS A MEDIATOR

STEP 1: Think back to occasions in the past when you were called upon to mediate or naturally stepped into this role. Have you ever been a mediator in your professional life, even if that wasn't technically part of your job description? Were you ever a mediator between family members or friends? You might jot down some memorable occasions or phases in your life when you did a lot of mediation.

STEP 2: Sit with some of the following questions for reflection:

- What has your experience with acting as a mediator traditionally been like for you?
- Did people at times respect, acknowledge, and appreciate your skill? At other times did people take advantage?
- When did you have healthy boundaries and when did you have poor boundaries as a mediator? Are you more comfortable setting healthy boundaries professionally or personally?
- When have you received something for acting as a mediator that made it a worthwhile and nourishing experience for you? What would you like to receive more of in the future?
- Were there times in the past when you protected your empath heart by rescuing or being the referee? Play with your clairvoyance, or visual psychic pathway, and notice if any images of you in a black-and-white referee costume come to mind when thinking back to certain jobs or relationships, or notice if you see yourself racing around to put out emotional fires like an emergency rescuer.

> ## MANTRA
> I don't have to rescue or referee to protect my empath heart. Having healthy emotional boundaries is a much higher priority for me than being a mediator for others, and putting myself first is always an excellent means of empath protection.

Creating Healthy Space Around Emotions, Situations & Relationships

Creating space around a challenging emotion, situation, or relationship is a great way to protect your empath heart—and this practice can also be the path to deep healing. Creating space around something challenging is a form of engaging witnessing/observer mode. I first learned about this practice from Eckhart Tolle, and the effects, especially for an empath who is wired to feel so much, can be profound.

There can be a balancing act between *feeling* your emotions so you don't minimize them, and yet not *becoming* your emotions or being totally overwhelmed by them. Emotions are meant to be felt. Processing them is a way to lovingly show up for and nurture yourself, as well as a method of discerning the healing invitations buried within your emotions. Within the anger of betrayal can be an invitation to change your boundaries with someone else; within the sadness of loneliness can be the invitation to create more intimacy with others; and within the joy of accomplishment can be an invitation to keep prioritizing your dreams.

Creating space around challenging emotions isn't meant to be a method of side-stepping emotions, but rather a coping skill for sitting with them more intentionally and fully. Creating space can be especially helpful when:

- **Someone in your life is triggering you** regarding an issue you feel vulnerable around or strongly about. When you are triggered, you feel an intense, abrupt, negative wave of emotion that is overwhelming. An example might be a friend who just announced on social media that they got pregnant quickly and easily—meanwhile you have been trying to conceive, via a plethora of methods, and been unsuccessful for years.
- **Someone is triggering an old wound from the past**, like a coworker not allowing you sufficient time to polish and

put finishing touches on an important project and thus launching it haphazardly. This might trigger your control and perfectionism issues, stemming from rejection or abandonment during childhood.

▨ **You have to regularly interact with someone challenging**—like a boss who annoys you or an ex you share children with—who can create negative emotions like frustration and resentment in you.

▨ **A significant relationship is ending or shifting**, and time away from someone is necessary or healthy.

If you need space from a challenging emotion or situation or relationship of your own, try the technique of imagining that this were happening not to you, but to someone you know and like. What wise, compassionate advice would you give them—if you were feeling grounded and calm—and they came to you for an objective opinion? You can even imagine what a person you respect—like a therapist you once had, or an insightful colleague you once worked with, or even a straight-talking but sweet and wise celebrity you follow might tell you.

You occasionally need to create space around a situation or relationship by temporarily walking away from it emotionally, mentally, and energetically for a bit to reset yourself. You can do this by placing the situation or relationship inside your healing well, which we will create in the following exercise.

CREATE YOUR MAGICAL HEALING WELL

STEP 1: Picture your healing well. This is a real, magical place in the energetic realm, so make it look like a real, physical well. If you grew up on a farm or in a rural area, it might be a well you remember from childhood. It could be inspired by a picture or illustration of a well you saw in a book, or a beautiful wishing well you saw in a fantasy movie. Mine is a well you might stumble upon in a mythical fairy wood, made of mossy stone, with beautiful garlands of flowers and ivy curling around it. There's also a healing magical mist floating up from its depths. Feel free to borrow my image, and, as you work with your healing well over time, you might change its appearance in your mind or add more personal details, just like you play with the décor of a room.

STEP 2: Think of a situation or relationship you'd like some space and a break from. You might see the face of a friend who really hurt your feelings in your mind, or you might think of a job search that's gone on for months and become disappointing and difficult. Keep in mind that this is a temporary break that might only last a few hours, a day, or a week or two. If you have just broken up with someone and need some space from analyzing the past or from your very challenging emotions about that person, you might place them inside your healing well for much longer. Keep in mind that you can place someone or something in your healing well and still interact with them, like a former business partner who you are negotiating terms with.

STEP 3: Imagine pulling up a magical bucket—made of silver, gold, or beautiful crystals—from deep in your well. Say a quick prayer silently for healing as you name the situation or person you are putting inside. If you'd like, call on Archangel Raphael, the angel of healing, during your prayer. Then lower the bucket back into your healing well slowly, where it will marinate in loving, alchemical waters. You might peer down and picture that water as sparkling and pure, or give it a comforting color like soft pink or purple, or imagine it as glittery and bedazzled with magic power. The source for the spring of this well is Spirit, so there's nothing more you need to do right now. Let love and a higher power do the work for you.

STEP 4: If you have been keeping your eyes closed to better visualize this, imagine a bell that hangs near the top of your well. Now imagine yourself gently tapping the bell and hearing the twinkling sound closing out your ritual. Open your eyes. Notice if you feel any changes energetically or emotionally.

STEP 5: Go about your normal life, and whenever your mind goes to this situation or relationship, remind yourself that it's evolving and transforming in your healing well. Let a sense of peace wash over you. Your healing well is a great way to practice creating space around a relationship, surrendering a relationship, and asking for divine assistance with a relationship. You can place as much as you need to in your healing well at any given time—its healing waters and reserves of love and divine protection are bottomless.

STEP 6: Let some time pass—an afternoon, a day, a week, a month—and then check in on the issue by imagining your healing well, pulling up the magic bucket, and noticing how you feel about the issue or relationship now. How have your feelings evolved? How have they stayed the same? Do you have any helpful new insights? What clarity do you have now, that you didn't when you first placed this inside your well? Has Spirit been able to work any healing magic around this issue for you—like an improvement in someone's behavior toward you or an important resource showing up—since the time you placed it in your healing well?

MANTRA
Creating healthy space around an issue or relationship can be healing. My healing well is a real place where real magical, loving energies can work on any of my relationships, even my relationship with myself.

Expanding Your Energy

You are such a big, important energy on this planet! Yet at times you might make yourself small—like downplaying your emotions, talents, skills, wants, beliefs, or needs—to make others feel comfortable, validated, or inflated.

Empaths might make themselves small when:

- Sensing the cultural, workplace, social, or familial collective energy and that being themselves might make them stick out or be perceived as different in uncomfortable ways.
- Sensing that owning their talents and skills would make a colleague or friend feel insecure or jealous. (We covered this in the previous chapter on assertiveness.)
- Needing a coping skill in childhood because guardians weren't able to meet a child's survival or emotional needs.
- Picking up on the emotional overwhelm or physical exhaustion of their guardians as a sensitive child, and not wanting to burden anyone.
- Picking up on the fact that their needs or desires will create negative feelings or judgment in others, and not wanting to hurt anyone or feel difficult feelings secondhand.

I first heard about expanding your energy from my friend and fellow author Tess Whitehurst. Instead of shrinking themselves to protect against everyone else's energy and emotions, empaths can protect themselves by *expanding*. You can try this quickly as an energy-shielding technique by:

- Connecting to your energy body, which is attached to, but larger than, your physical body.
- Feeling the energy field coming from you with your clairsentient psychic pathway.

- Imagining your energy body pushing out into the air around you, several inches or several feet, and thickening, becoming bigger as well as denser.
- Imagining that your energy body has a color, shape, or texture if that's helpful.

Another simple way to expand your energy is by prioritizing yourself! We'll practice doing this in the next exercise by working with your inner child and giving yourself what you craved more of in childhood. When you learn to better show up for yourself and meet your own needs, it can protect you from trying to get your needs met via unhealthy relationships.

GIVE YOURSELF NOW WHAT YOU CRAVED MORE OF AS A CHILD

STEP 1: Identify what you craved more of as a child. These might be real *things*, like survival needs such as clothing, money, and food, or other physical items like books, musical instruments, sporting equipment, and toys. Maybe you craved companionship, like more friends or pets or siblings, or more community, like being a more active member of your town, school, club, team, or church. You might have craved more stability, like more routine or a grounding physical home. What did you crave emotionally that seemed in short supply in the environments you grew up in—fun, unconditional love, connection, visibility, gentle touch, wisdom, humor, healthy discipline, protection, encouragement, or nurturing? What kind of energy was lacking in your childhood—playful energy, responsible energy, caretaking energy, or secure energy?

STEP 2: Activate your loving inner parent, a concept I learned about from my friend Natasha Levinger, author of *Healing Your Inner Child*. Give your inner parent a name, physical description, and personality, or imagine them like someone you admire and would consider a dream parent, such as Oprah or Mr. Rogers. Remember that showing up for your own inner child isn't about judging and shaming your real-life parents or guardians, although this exercise might bring up anger, sadness, or any other feeling about your childhood or one of your caretakers. If that happens, enlist your loving inner parent to seek out extra emotional support for yourself.

STEP 3: Lovingly parent yourself by picking three to five things (physical objects, emotional experiences, nurturing energies) that you craved more of as a child, and prioritizing them in your life right now.

Keep in mind that giving to your inner child does not have to look a certain way, like growing up in impoverished circumstances and now being wealthy, or growing up feeling isolated and now having tons of friends, family, colleagues, and community. Simply find a way to show up for your inner child, engaging your loving inner parent and offering what your inner child craved back then in any healthy way you're able to now as an adult. Very small ways can often be enormously healing. Simply the fact that you're acknowledging your inner child is healing!

> **MANTRA**
> Expanding my energy creates an expansive feeling of security and love inside me. I don't have to become small to be safe or loved.

Grounding with Earth Energy

Most empaths who've come to me for intuitive readings over the years are big nature lovers. Taking a safe walk in a park, watching the sunset from your porch, or listening to waves lapping the beach can soothe an empath's sensitive heart. Why is nature so calming and grounding for empaths? Because empaths can instantly tune in to all the nature elements around them: the free, expansive energy of a wide-open sky; the stable, rooted energy of a mighty tree; or the gentle, playful energy of a flower in full bloom. Empaths can possess a mutable energy capable of easily matching to just about anything around them, and a nature scene on a calm, beautiful day is fabulous energy to piggyback on!

There's something incredibly grounding about the energy of nature, and feeling grounded is one of the best energy-protection methods around. When you're grounded, your energy is centered, as opposed to being scattered. Being grounded—or feeling calm, present, and secure—makes it much easier to control where your energy goes and to choose what energies outside yourself you want to let in or not.

Yet you don't have to live near a pristine beach or own a private forest to benefit from nature's bountiful, grounding energy. In *Self-Care for Empaths*, I talked about aligning to the earth's energy by pulling it up into your own energy body. An easy way to do this is through your feet. You probably already do this unconsciously any time you take a walk outside, but you can do it more mindfully by standing on some river rocks, standing barefoot in the sand or grass, or even standing in your home or on the sidewalk and connecting to the earth energy below your feet. Just thinking about the chakras, or energy centers, on the bottoms of your feet will activate them.

In the next exercise, we'll practice grounding by resetting your own energy to Earth time, which happens one minute, and one breath, at a time.

RESET YOUR INTERNAL CLOCK
TO EARTH TIME

STEP 1: Pick a few hours—a lazy Sunday evening, a weekday afternoon at work or home when there's not much that's pressing on the agenda—to reset your internal clock to Earth time.

STEP 2: Simply slow down. Avoid setting your internal clock to modern time and its inclination to rush through the day.

- If you eat a meal, chew your food more mindfully, noticing all the subtle flavors and textures.
- If you have to pick up children's toys, take your time with the task, and let a fun or frustratingly funny memory linger in your mind with every piece of joy you put back on the shelf or in the toy chest.
- If you're taking a shower, stay present as you lather up with soap, soaking in all the sensory details like the squishy, soft feel of the soap against your skin, the smell of your shampoo in your hair, and the sight of the steam in the air.

Purposefully move more slowly through these hours so you can feel more present. Earth time happens one second at a time; and when you move more slowly and intentionally through your day, those seconds tend to stretch and feel like they last even longer. You might find that by moving slower, you're not only able to savor your day more, you get more done!

STEP 3: Be mindful of your breath. It's common that in a rush-rush world, everything begins to feel like an emergency—even running errands like going to the grocery store after work. You might be rushing around the aisles, grabbing anything, hoping you can still get home in time to relax a bit before bed and the whole daily cycle of work and chores and responsibilities begins again. Empaths easily tune in to collective energy, and digital, modern-day energy is very fast-moving, as quick and instantaneous as a site loading onto your computer screen. Rushing puts your body on red alert, in a state of fight-flight-freeze. Your breathing might become more rapid and shallow, or you might even find yourself holding your breath. Reminding your body that it's safe by taking calm, steady, full breaths helps reset your nervous system from overdrive to neutral—Earth time is more neutral and balanced. When your breath is calm, it's a similar feeling to sitting outside in nature on a beautiful day.

STEP 4: Work with these two techniques—slowing down and being intentional with your breath—any time your automatic pilot is set to red alert, or life is moving too fast, or you are stressed. Resetting to Earth time is an ideal way to quickly, easily reset your sensitive empath nervous system.

> ## MANTRA
> I can reset my energy any time by grounding in to nature or by aligning with Earth time. Simply slowing down and being mindful of my breath protects my sensitive system from the collective energy of a rush-rush world.

Surrendering Instead of Clutching Others

An empath's ability to intimately share in someone else's experience and emotions enables intense bonding with others. No doubt there are friends, family members, and colleagues who mean the world to you, and as an empath you also have a pronounced ability to empathize with people you know only casually or even people who are strangers. Because of this, empaths might instinctively clutch at someone else's emotions or *experience* without realizing that that's what they're doing.

To *clutch* means to grasp and hold tightly. In fashion, a clutch is a small purse that someone holds on to all evening at a formal event. As a clotheshorse, I'm all in favor of clutching a fabulous accessory! As far as clutching people, I'd like you to avoid that, or be more mindful of it.

Clutching looks like:

    ▓ **Worrying about someone else all the time,** or
       continually trying to problem-solve someone else's issues
       in your mind.

- **Attempting to control or manage someone else's experience** by insisting you know what's best for them, or trying to talk them out of their emotions.
- **Only feeling calm or happy in relation to others**, like if the people closest to you are calm, happy, or "okay."
- **Always wondering what someone else is feeling or doing**, as if you are on hold and your life is simply trying to anticipate them.
- **Reacting to the needs and desires of others**, as opposed to proactively meeting your own needs and desires.
- **Being hyperaware of what others expect from you**, and treating those expectations as your top priority.
- **Feeling like someone won't be okay** without you.
- **Fixating** on your desire for someone to be or act differently.

Practicing the art of surrender can aid empaths when they realize they're clutching someone else.

Surrendering looks like:

- **Reminding yourself that everyone is on their own path**, and that all you can control is your own behavior.
- **Acknowledging that you may not always know** what's best for others.
- **Stepping back** to let others find their own answers, truths, or way.
- **Giving your advice when it's asked for**, or when you feel called to do so, but then releasing your attachment to people acting on your advice.
- **Trying to love unconditionally**—other people and yourself.
- **Pulling back** from someone if being very close is unhealthy.

■ Trusting that there are other forces besides yourself to help meet someone else's needs and desires.

Surrendering is about practice, not perfection. Every relationship is different, and every circumstance is different. With a certain loved one, you might surrender your desire for them to get help managing their obsessive-compulsive disorder, and with another loved one you might hold an intervention to try and get them help for a drug addiction. Similarly, you might tell a nosy colleague exactly what you think of their meddling before you surrender, but with an in-law you might decide to bite your tongue and surrender immediately when they begin gossiping at a holiday gathering.

Surrender is always there as a tool to help you protect your empath heart. Use your own best judgment for how and when to implement surrender. One of the best methods I know for letting go of someone else is coming home to your own energy, emotions, and experience, which we'll practice next.

COME HOME TO YOURSELF

STEP 1: The next time you catch yourself clutching on to someone else's energy, emotions, and experience, find a few minutes to go to a quiet place alone. Connect with your physical body by getting comfortable, like adjusting your chair, eating a snack, drinking water, going to the bathroom, or doing whatever will help your body settle and relax.

STEP 2: Take a deep breath, and put your hand over your heart. Give yourself sixty seconds to breathe and just rest with your hand over your physical heart to tune in to your energetic heart.

STEP 3: Now silently ask yourself, "What's going on with me?" Let this question bring you back to your life, your experience, your emotions, your energy. You might realize you feel anxious or tired, happy or calm, full or hungry. If your mind tries to bring in someone else, just keep coming home to you, not how you relate to others.

STEP 4: Then ask yourself, "How can I support myself right now?" You might realize you need a nap or a break, or that you're excited about a creative project and want to spend more time working on it. Come up with a quick, simple action step to support yourself, like scheduling an afternoon off if you realize you're overwhelmed, or reaching out to a friend if you realize you'd love to hang out and have fun.

STEP 5: Use this quick exercise to come home to yourself any time you are entangled in someone else's energy. If you're ever struggling to know immediately how to support yourself, or even what you're feeling, step away from the exercise and ask your intuition to let you know the answer over the next twenty-four hours in words, thoughts, pictures, or feelings.

> **MANTRA**
> When I find myself clutching on to others, the quickest path to healthy release and surrender is coming home to my own energy, emotions, and experience. Clutching is for purses, not people!

Not Judging Very Judgmental People

Do you know some very judgmental colleagues, friends, and family members? Whose face or name comes to mind when I ask that question? Whether the judgmental person believes they are enforcing the "correct" behavior, just trying to "help," or simply "passing on some interesting information" (usually passive-aggressively judging), empaths may not like to see others judged, as it's a harsh energy that impacts people in damaging ways. I even had a hard time writing this section, as I truly don't want to judge judgmental people. We all need to be held accountable for our actions, and ethical standards are essential in society. But what I'm referring to is the person who is always gossiping, always making others "wrong," always hard to please, and often has a lot of difficulty taking constructive criticism themselves.

Knowing that someone in your life—like a boss who always finds fault but rarely offers praise, or a relative who seems impossible to please—is generally more judgmental and critical is so powerful! Sometimes awareness is the best protection, allowing you to meet another person's criticism or judgment in witnessing/observer mode, so you can put healthy, protective emotional space around their opinions of you and others.

Have trouble mustering up compassion for very judgmental people? Remember that people often treat themselves the way they treat others. If an old friend is supercritical of your new career, they are probably pretty critical of themselves internally. Set boundaries with judgmental people about what they can and cannot say to you, and, when you can muster it, do so with compassion. You are likely dealing with an incredibly insecure adult who was raised in a very judgmental, hypercritical culture or family.

When I think back to times in my own life when I was very judgmental, I summon compassion for myself by remembering that those were also times when I was struggling a lot internally, feeling very resentful or unhappy about aspects of my life. If a period from your own life when you were especially critical of yourself or others comes to mind right now, call up an image of yourself back then and send that past self some love and TLC. Oh, how they needed it! This nurturing energy helps heal that older version of you that's still somewhere inside you.

It's natural to judge others and even ourselves *to a degree.* Yet constantly judging or criticizing others displays poor boundaries, as it involves leaving your own emotions and experience and inserting yourself aggressively into someone else's sacred space. When trying to neutralize a challenging energy, like judgment, don't mirror it. Instead, meet it with a different energy.

CREATE ENERGY INSTEAD OF MIRRORING IT

STEP 1: If reading the previous section immediately brought some extra-critical people in your life to mind, use one of them for this exercise. You can also ask your intuition to show you through words, pictures, thoughts, or feelings who to concentrate on for this exercise, or you might experience a synchronicity—a meaningful coincidence—like someone calling, texting, or emailing you as you are reading this section or thinking about this section of the book.

STEP 2: Practice creating healthy space around this person's criticisms and judgments. When they speak, or when you read their words in a text or email, imagine a soft cloud of pink energy surrounding, buffering, and protecting you, or imagine their words coming from very far away, like the bottom of a hill or the end of a long hallway.

STEP 3: When you address them, use a calm, gentle tone and choose words that are neutral and, if appropriate, soothing. In this way you are also *softening* the energy instead of mirroring their harsh energy.

STEP 4: If someone's consistent judgmental, critical attitude is causing damage to you or others, consider how you can set tighter boundaries with them as well, like letting them know what type of comments are acceptable and unacceptable. You may even decide you need to pull away from them.

STEP 5: When this person's judgments or criticisms come to mind later, run them through your heart filter. Place your hand over your heart, and ask yourself if any part of what they said might be useful. Then put the same information in the context of compassion, and imagine someone very loving and gentle telling the information to you in a kinder, softer way.

STEP 6: Model compassion for very judgmental people to create energy instead of mirroring it. Empathize with yourself or others verbally or demonstratively so the judgmental person can see what that looks like. Compassionate criticism might be a new concept for them! Humans tend to unconsciously mirror the energy around them, so just by modeling compassion you might find that a judgmental person's energy begins to soften around you as they mirror your energy. This is an empath Jedi mind trick!

> ### MANTRA
> Knowing that I need to protect myself around very judgmental people is powerful. I don't have to mirror someone else's challenging energy. Instead, I can meet them with a different energy, like the energy of healthy boundaries or compassion—or both.

Stabilizing Your Energy by Stabilizing Your Life

When your energy is stable—you're feeling relatively calm, secure, and present—it's much easier to protect yourself from all the energetic and emotional fluctuations around you. That's because when your energy is centered and focused, it's stronger, so your natural energy defenses are stronger too.

Highs and lows of other individuals, or collective energy, won't affect an empath as much when they can better regulate their own energy. Luckily, you don't need to do anything fancy or unusual, like search the earth for the perfect crystal, or scour the Internet for the perfect shielding meditation, to stabilize your energy. While those tools can be very useful or powerful for some people, what I find more useful and powerful myself—and what I recommend to empath clients—is straight-up, old-school, stabilizing self-care.

If you're feeling drained, scattered, or anxious, and you suspect that part of the issue might be your sensitivity and picking up on the energy and emotions around you, try stabilizing your life even more. Stabilizing practices include:

- **Keeping your finances in check.** When possible, try not to overextend yourself financially, so that you have enough money to meet your monthly bills and some savings to fall back on in emergencies.
- **Regulating your blood sugar.** Try to consume sweets—which can even include high-glycemic carbs and fruits—in moderation. Eat healthy snacks throughout the day and drink clean water. If there are certain natural supplements or certain medications that help keep your blood sugar stable, be sure to take them regularly.
- **Stabilizing your relationship to stimulants and depressants.** Some empaths might find that their sensitive nervous systems react more strongly to depressants like alcohol or stimulants like coffee. Using them in moderation, or abstaining, will help.
- **Stabilizing your living situation.** As someone who had a very unstable living situation from the ages of fifteen to nineteen (I lived in eight different homes and apartments during that period, the majority of which were very unstable and precarious), I know firsthand the value of home. Keep in mind that home can be a temporary place,

and often is. Try to find a living situation where you feel reasonably safe, supported, and secure, so you can settle in, whether that's for months or years.

■ **Developing nourishing routines.** Simple daily routines can do wonders to calm your sensitive nervous system, like eating your meals at the same times, going to bed and getting up at roughly the same times, making your bed in the morning, pulling an oracle card for inspiration, showering, meditating, praying, calling a loved one on your lunch break, walking your dog after work, or reading before bed. The calming, emotionally stabilizing effect of routine is why experts often recommend keeping small children on regimented daily schedules. If one of your daily routines gets boring, switch things up! Weekly routines—like a weekly family/ friend dinner, weekly yoga class, or weekly meeting of a spiritual community—as well as monthly routines, can be incredibly grounding.

■ **Supporting your overall health.** Much like everything else in life—finances, living situation, relationships, career—your health may be always shifting. You may be managing chronic health issues, or you might be recovering from an injury or temporary illness. Do what you can to help stabilize your health, which might include avoiding unnecessary stress, getting enough sleep, gentle exercise, and eating a healthy diet. If you suspect you have gut-health issues, vitamin and mineral deficiencies, thyroid issues, or a hormone imbalance (I went through a decade-long healing journey where I dealt with all these and more), reach out to a health-care professional for guidance. Whether it's achy joints or a change in your vision, make sure you're getting all the help your body needs and deserves.

■ **Seeking out balanced emotional support.** Sensitive people might isolate to try and regulate their systems and control the amount of outside energies and emotions they absorb. While I advocate for regular retreat-and-recovery time for empaths, I also know that being in regular relationship to others is very healthy and necessary. No one was meant to celebrate life's joys and shoulder its burdens alone. Whether with a trusted counselor, a caring friend, or a gentle family member—or all of these—sharing your emotional experience can dramatically help stabilize your emotions and energy.

SUMMON COURAGE TO MAKE CHANGES WITH ARCHANGEL MICHAEL

STEP 1: In the previous passage, I offered seven different areas of your life to work on stabilizing. Ask your intuition for a number between 1 and 7 in words, images, or thoughts. (When I did this, I heard the number "5" in my mind, and also saw a mental image of the number 5.)

STEP 2: Based on your intuition's recommendation, or whatever area of your life you feel most drawn to or is most pressing, develop an action plan for stabilizing this area of your life even more. My intuition recommended I work on number 5, or developing nourishing routines. Remember that baby steps count! Sometimes when you take one small, manageable action step, the next best action step becomes obvious, and soon a path to healthy change begins magically forming. The universe will always try to support healthy change, so notice if grace, in the form of helpful people or opportunities or resources, begins showing up.

STEP 3: Change—even when it's positive—can be inherently scary, triggering, or challenging. If you need to summon courage to begin taking action to stabilize an area of your life, call on Archangel Michael. Known as the protector of the angel realm, Michael is a dedicated advocate and warrior who specializes in stabilizing energy and can help you summon your inner reserve of courage. Simply call on Michael in your thoughts, write a few lines in your journal to Michael, or create a mental picture of a magnificent angel with large feather wings. If you are very sensitive to energy, you might at times feel a palpable energy shift when you call on Michael, as I just did in my office while writing this exercise.

STEP 4: In addition to spiritual support, reach out to helpful humans for support. The support of a group, a friend, or a counselor or other health-care professional can be invaluable when changing your habits and patterns.

If angels don't resonate with you, call on an ancestor who was brave and courageous, or channel the energy of someone in the public eye or history who you associate with bravery and courage, like Tina Turner, simply by thinking of them. Being sensitive and receptive to energy as an empath, you have a gift for channeling energy!

> ## MANTRA
> The more I can stabilize the major aspects of my life, the more my energy will settle, stabilize, and strengthen. Since I cannot control everything, I work on stabilizing what I can.

Mindfully Adjusting Your Level of Vulnerability & Intimacy in a Relationship

Empaths can bond very quickly with others. An empath's ability to read another person and feel what they are feeling can at times make others feel understood, seen, and comfortable early on in a relationship. This is one of the many blessings of being a sensitive person—a unique talent for connecting in meaningful ways with other humans!

Relationships evolve organically, yet when you find yourself either becoming very close with someone or needing to pull away from someone, it's helpful to do that mindfully. Getting close to others involves being a lot more vulnerable. As you share more of yourself and become more available to someone, people get a window into all of you: everything you're proud of, comfortable with, and celebrate about yourself, and also the wounded, insecure, and tender parts of you. This is why some people fear intimacy and pull quickly out of relationships that, to the person they were in the relationship with, seemed to be going really well—a giant fear of exposing their underbelly.

To become very intimate with someone is to show them your underbelly, or the part of you that's most vulnerable and easily hurt. When dogs feel very comfortable and safe around someone, they will often roll over so that person can pet their underbelly. Back when my brother was looking for a shelter dog to adopt, the shelter worker told him, "I want to show you a special dog. He always growls at people, and we are having a very hard time placing him. We believe he was severely abused, but I want to find a loving home and a new chapter for him."

My brother agreed to meet this dog, and within minutes the dog was wagging his tail and flipping over to expose his underbelly to my brother. The worker from the shelter was stunned. "I've never seen him do that before!" My brother immediately adopted that very special dog.

Sometimes you just get a feeling about someone very early in your relationship with them—as my brother did with this shelter dog. Always listen to your intuition, because as a sensitive person you have a pronounced access to your sixth sense. Being mindful involves using the strategic, practical side of your brain, and you really should have both—your intuitive and practical senses—online and active when establishing intimacy with others. We get the best out of relationships when we open up fully to others, as the shelter dog did with my brother. Yet opening up fully is also when we can feel the most pain.

With all our new, and even old, relationships, it's good to periodically do a little inventory of how we feel around a person. Are they someone who is caring, and who supports and celebrates you? If so, you might want to invest even more time and energy in this relationship, and allow the intimacy to deepen and mature. On the other hand, sometimes a new colleague or old friend can be going through a phase where they aren't as caring and supportive, or might be overly critical of you. If so, you can mindfully pull back your level of intimacy with them temporarily, and see if the situation improves. Other times, you might suddenly realize that an old or new friend is actually quite self-centered and even narcissistic, and the adjustment in your level of intimacy could be permanent.

The downside of bonding quickly with others is that an empath may stay in a relationship, or at a certain level of intimacy with someone, simply because they don't want to disappoint, hurt, or abandon the other person. These sentiments could be true of any compassionate human; yet for the empath who feels in their own system what other people feel, it can be an even more intense experience to consider pulling away. An empath might actually try to *protect* themselves from a relationship that needs to end by staying. This seems counterintuitive, but it stops an empath from having to feel their own tender compassion toward another hurting person, as well as feeling secondhand that person's challenging emotions created by the split.

It's great to remember that not all relationships end or change abruptly. More often, especially with friends and colleagues, relationships can gradually transform into a lesser degree of closeness and intimacy, just as they can also slowly deepen and mature into more intimacy and closeness.

Mindfully getting closer and more intimate can look like:

- Noticing that you enjoy thinking about this person.
- Prioritizing time with them or interacting with them.
- Realizing that sharing in their concerns and joys feels connecting and nourishing.
- Admiring them or reflecting that you learn new things and look at life in new ways, thanks to them.
- Looking forward to spending time with them.
- Feeling safe to be vulnerable around them.
- Noticing that they display compassion and honesty, are self-reflective, and have a sense of their strengths and weaknesses or a sense of humor about themselves.
- Feeling deep compassion for them when their underbellies—or the vulnerable, wounded, and insecure parts—are revealed.
- Observing that you feel at home or relaxed around them, or that you can be your authentic self.
- Realizing that they bring out new sides of you, challenge you in healthy ways, or that the relationship is helping you heal and evolve.
- Being thankful that they encourage you with your larger goals or dreams.
- Letting the other person know in your words and actions that you appreciate and value them, and having them reciprocate in turn.

Mindfully pulling back from someone can look like:

- Curating how much space they occupy in your thoughts.
- Setting tighter boundaries on how much time you spend with them.
- Noticing that hearing from them can sometimes make you feel annoyed, resentful, or burdened.

- Keeping things back from them in conversation because you don't feel safe and supported being vulnerable with them.
- Diplomatically letting them know if they say or do things that you consider unkind, inappropriate, or unhealthy.
- Recognizing that you may not have as much in common anymore.
- Noticing that you don't seem to strengthen, push, or challenge each other in positive ways, or that you can be catty and dismissive with each other.
- Realizing that issues you have with each other seem stagnant instead of improving or evolving.
- Becoming unable to muster up genuine sympathy for their tender underbelly.
- Wondering if you have outgrown each other, or if the deep intimacy and growth you once shared has served its purpose in both your lives.
- Wanting to make space for new people and new experiences.
- Not making the other person wrong or bad, just concluding that they're not as compatible with what you're currently craving in a friend, lover, colleague, or close family member as you'd like.
- Possibly feeling intense gratitude for the closeness you once shared in the past, and wanting to honor that in some way now.

Decreasing or increasing intimacy mindfully and intentionally will help you better support yourself, and help you avoid acting out in unconscious or self-sabotaging ways, during the process. Sometimes a relationship simply needs some space to heal and recalibrate, or requires a bigger intimacy investment from you to grow in cool, new ways. However the relationship evolves, or even if you decide to end it, mindfully increasing or decreasing intimacy will help you make a more clear-headed decision.

PERFORM A RELATIONSHIP INVENTORY & SET UP INTIMACY SPEED BUMPS

STEP 1: Choose a relationship in your life that feels like it's changing or evolving. It might be a business partnership that feels stagnant or a personal relationship that is becoming more important to you.

STEP 2: Ask yourself the following questions:

1. What have I learned or gained from the relationship thus far? What am I hoping for, going forward?
2. Have the other person and I experienced any significant personal growth or healing from the relationship?
3. Does this relationship seem to have plateaued, or is it still actively growing? If this is a long-term relationship, have we experienced cycles of less and more intimacy and closeness before?
4. Am I happy and satisfied with the relationship as it is, or am I longing for a change in the dynamic?
5. If the other person's feelings, and other outside factors, weren't an issue, would I want to spend more, or less, time with this person?
6. If this relationship were a financial investment, would I consider it a winning strategy I'm satisfied with and want to invest more in, or would I be looking for new opportunities?
7. Does this relationship fulfill some of my major needs and desires? If not, what does it fulfill?
8. What drew me to this person? Why do I believe they came into my life?
9. Am I shy and reserved about showing my underbelly to this person, or is sharing with them nourishing? Either way, why might this be so?

10. What intuitive signals am I getting from them about the relationship? Does the other person seem to be pulling away, or wanting to go deeper? How do I feel about that—uncomfortable, excited, content, disappointed?
11. What is my energy like when I'm around this person or thinking of them—is it open and relaxed, or is it tight and closed off? What other descriptive words could I use?
12. Is there another relationship from my past that *this* relationship reminds me of?

STEP 3: Consult a trusted loved one or counselor. Sometimes you can subtly shift the intimacy level with someone, either increasing or decreasing it, and other times you might need to be more straightforward.

STEP 4: If you've gotten close to someone very quickly, and it's feeling overwhelming or too intense, place some strategic speed bumps on the road to vulnerability. These are also great tools if you are wanting to create a little healthy space between you and someone who might be becoming less important in your life.

- **Make yourself less available.** Sometimes quality time is better than quantity time—even when you really, really enjoy someone—especially for sensitive empaths who love to have their space! This also includes making your mind less available, taking your thoughts to other topics outside this person.
- **Practice witnessing/observer mode with this person.** Instead of always opening up to feel with them, be mindful of staying in your own energy and emotions around them.
- **Take a beat before you agree to plans or the other person's agenda.** When looking to mindfully increase your intimacy with others, it can be fun to adopt an

adventurous, playful, "yes" attitude. When you're wanting to pull away from a relationship that is draining, or just to create healthy space when a fun relationship is progressing very quickly, practice saying "no" with love.

■ **Prioritize healthy alone time and time with other people.** Invest in quality solo retreat-and-recover time, like attending a weekend workshop alone. Ask an acquaintance out to lunch and invest in some budding relationships that show potential for growth, or connect with an old friend or colleague you miss.

> ### MANTRA
> I can have various degrees of vulnerability with different people at different times. As an empath whose sensitivity makes me naturally very open, mindfully adjusting my level of intimacy is a great protection mechanism.

Liberating the Shining Star Within You

We all have a bright star inside that longs to shine out into the world. Usually this is the part of you with a unique talent or skill that is uniquely suited to helping others. Every human, and every empath, has special gifts. You might be especially good at storytelling, parenting, math, playing the piano, brainstorming, basketball, counseling, languages, critical thinking, carpentry, visual art, healing, teaching, caretaking, gardening, mechanics, or showing others unconditional compassion. While every human has special gifts inside that are designed to help others, sometimes empaths have trouble feeling okay about shining their gifts out into the world. They might try to dim their glow, or stay small, to protect themselves.

Because empaths are so sensitive, they are sensitive to the opinions of others. You might have a coworker who is secretly jealous of or threatened by you and encourages you not to shine at the office. Perhaps someone in your family was raised in a household or culture that encouraged people not to shine, and they shame you for trying to share your gifts. Or you might meet someone who simply doesn't value what you have to offer. In their opinion, the way you shine isn't worthy of sharing.

Some people are so confident and centered that they can shrug off or quickly put into perspective someone else's very diminishing opinion of them. Empaths are so sensitive to the viewpoints of other people that they may start to relate to someone else's diminishing opinion of them. Empaths are natural diplomats, because they can tune in to others and easily understand why someone else feels as they do. However, this talent was never meant to keep you from shining.

Empaths might be able to quickly resonate with the idea that everyone is equally important, simply because they can equally feel everyone. So perhaps as an empath you have turned the dimmer on your sparkle so as not to appear more important than anyone else. Or maybe you hide your shine around some people, sensing intuitively that the way you shine in the world is hard for them—because they haven't yet figured out how to shine, don't appreciate their own sparkle, or haven't figured out what you feel so immediately . . . that we are all equally worthy.

Because empaths can often be so compassionate, they love to help others. Letting your inner star shine is about discerning your unique gifts and sharing them to be of greater service. It can also be a way to inspire others to shine!

CONNECT WITH STAR ENERGY

STEP 1: Find a safe place to go or look outside—like in your back yard, on your front porch, or out your window—on a clear night.

STEP 2: Look up into the night sky and find a twinkling star you can focus on.

STEP 3: As you admire this star's brilliance, spend a few minutes contemplating the ways you are brilliant!

- What natural gifts do you possess?
- What skills have you honed over time?
- And most important, how can your own brilliance light others up, help them, teach them, bring them joy, offer them more meaning, or help heal them?

STEP 4: Make a wish on this star, just like when you were a kid (if you still make wishes on stars, you are an empath after my own empath heart). Then think back to when you *were* a kid. Ponder these questions:

- What did you want to be when you grew up?
- What were you excited to go out and experience in the world when you were younger?
- As a child or teen, what did you love to spend your time doing?
- Back then, were there supportive adults—like teachers, neighbors, or guardians—who made comments about what might be your gifts? In hindsight, which comments seem like wise observations of your soul?

STEP 5: If getting comfortable with letting your inner star shine is something you are working on, consider incorporating the symbol of a star into your daily life. Get a suncatcher crystal in the shape of a star, buy a scarf with a big star on it, make the image of a twinkly outer-space sky the screen saver on your phone or computer, or create a bottle of glittery stardust.

> **MANTRA**
> It's healthy for me to shine. My unique brilliance can make the world a better place.

Discerning When to Open, and When to Protect, Your Empath Heart

Opening up to feel with others is an incredibly nourishing experience, and one that sensitive empaths are naturally wired for! Whether you are feeling with people who are struggling, or people who are thriving, opening up to feel is an expansive energy that brings your sensitive energetic heart alive. Connection is something all humans crave, including empaths.

If you're going through a lot emotionally yourself—like feeling really high and excited about your life, or feeling really confused and fragile about your situation—it might be better to protect your empath heart from feeling so much with others. Feeling especially drained, scattered, or anxious can all be signs that it might be best to raise the drawbridge to your energetic heart and mindfully witness and observe others instead of feeling with them.

Opening up to feel with others can be ideal when:

- You're feeling calm, grounded, and centered.
- Giving and showing up for others is something you're yearning to do.
- The stress and drama levels in your own life are low or minimal.
- You're feeling disconnected, isolated, or lonely.
- You are physically rested and have good physical stamina.
- Sharing in someone else's joy, pain, or neutral experience can inform your own experience, healing, understanding, or growth.
- Your intuition strongly guides you to feel with someone.

Protecting your sensitive empath heart can be ideal when:

- You've been going through a lot emotionally lately— whether it involves a transition, a tragedy, a miracle, or just more emotional engagement.

- You find yourself wanting to retreat and recover because you're overwhelmed or overstimulated as a sensitive person, or you're craving alone time to connect with your own experience, emotions, and energy.
- You've been supporting others emotionally a lot lately.
- Opening up to feel with someone is not your immediate intuitive instinct, or you find yourself automatically going into witnessing/observer mode.
- A person who is feeling intensely good or bad comes to you for connection, and you sense that the best way to support them is to stay in a calm, grounded space.
- What someone else is going through triggers one of your own past wounds, and your emotions or physical body tell you it's too much to feel with them at the moment.
- You're feeling with someone and it becomes overwhelming or unsettling.

The morning I sat down in my office to write this section, I experienced a powerful synchronicity. Scanning the daily headlines, I noticed one about a painful anniversary—the deaths of several young women decades ago. I realized I remembered the awful event in the news cycle, way back when, even though at the time I was only seventeen years old.

It was a story that made national headlines, and some of the beautiful, sweet, innocent young women who lost their lives had been the same age as me at the time of the tragedy, and had eerily similar life circumstances. It made me think way back then, when the story broke, "That could have been me." I had the same feeling sitting in my office thirty years later.

Yet it hadn't been me. I'd gone on to have thirty more years of life (so far). What tore at my heart was the thought of these tender young women from the news story, who had been robbed of decades, decades that I had been able to keep living, loving, growing, and experiencing. I thought of their families. As tears came to my eyes, I wondered, what do I do now?

I had two choices—I could go into these feelings and give these young women and their loved ones some space in my heart, or I could take my mind elsewhere, engage my witnessing/observer mode, and come back to my work and my day. Yet I sensed intuitively that this story had become part of my work and my day.

Because I was feeling calm and grounded, I had no stressful deadlines and no clients to show up for in sessions that day, and was experiencing no personal drama of my own, I made the mindful decision to open up and feel into these lives and events.

I looked at the young women's pictures, read their parents' lovely descriptions of their personalities, and researched the advocacy groups that were making meaningful changes to protect others like them—in the names of these precious young women. Their lives had been short, but their families were making sure that these young women would have a long, impactful, healing legacy.

I thought back to how I felt unprotected in so many ways at that age, yet how I survived, and was so, so very grateful. Suddenly those years as a young adult and grown woman felt so amazingly precious. I had a renewed sense of purpose about trying to help keep the young people in my life and community safe and well, and I felt moved to take action on issues in my personal life that had been causing me to feel frozen—I wanted to embrace the gift of life and live more fully.

Connecting with the memory of these young women and feeling into their story had been so meaningful and healing for me. As I wrapped up my workday I thought of the vigil that would be held that evening in their memory. I wrapped a scarf around myself, sat in my back yard, and lit a candle to honor their memory. I sat in silence, looking at the stark yet beautiful winter landscape, and sent those souls who had passed—safe from harm now and forever—and their families my love and any healing energy I had access to.

We'll talk more about opening up to feel mindfully in another chapter, yet I wanted to include this story here, in the protection chapter, as a reminder that protecting yourself as an empath is not always the most nourishing option. Your sensitive heart longs to do what it's designed for— feeling with others. It's also important to know how to disconnect and release someone else's emotions and energies when you have been commingled, which we'll practice in the next exercise.

COCOON TO CALM, RELEASE & RECENTER

STEP 1: Cocooning as a sensitive person means to buffer yourself from too much stimulation from the outside world—just as a caterpillar is encased and protected in a cocoon during a vulnerable stage. You can slip into the neutral, calm energy of cocooning almost any time, almost anywhere. First, just make the conscious decision to cocoon.

STEP 2: If you've been feeling a lot with others, or absorbing a lot of stimuli from the outside world (like being in a bustling workplace or school all day), remind yourself that you are now switching gears and coming home to yourself. Take some deep breaths and remind yourself to slow down and calm down. Make your immediate environment as gentle, comfortable, and low stimulation as possible—soft lighting, soft music, comfortable clothes, comfortable place to lie, sit, stand, or walk.

STEP 3: Take your thoughts and focus to a neutral, pleasant subject that is interesting to you and not emotionally charged. If you just got off the phone with a friend who is excited about their big, happy personal news and you were feeling the joy and thrill with them, or you just left a meeting at work where management was hand-wringing over next year's budget and you were feeling the frustration and pressure, take your thoughts to something different and less intense. Like the interesting documentary you watched last night, or the fascinating character in the novel you're reading. Or get lost in an engaging activity like a creative hobby or house project you are itching to spend time on. Remember, where your thoughts and focus go, your energy flows.

STEP 4: Every time your mind wants to go back to the person you were feeling with, or tries to process all the stimulation you were absorbing, remind yourself that you are cocooning. Gently take your thoughts and focus back to the interesting and neutral subject you are pondering, the soft music you are listening to, or the gentle activity you are currently engaged in. Notice what your five physical senses are experiencing, like the feel of the cushion you're resting on or the smell of aromatherapy in the room or the colors of the dishes you are washing, to anchor you in the present moment.

STEP 5: Now that you have practiced cocooning to release someone else's energy—like the difficult coworker you can't stop thinking about, or the new romantic interest you need to stop daydreaming about so you can get some work done—cocoon on a regular basis. Maybe lazy Saturday afternoons are a regular cocooning opportunity on your calendar, or evenings after chores are done and young children are put to bed. Your favorite hobbies and activities—like hiking, gardening, reading a fantasy novel, cooking—might already be some of your go-to cocooning strategies.

> ### MANTRA
> It's not a perfect science, but I can exercise more control and choice about either opening up to feel or protecting my empath heart. If I've been absorbing a lot from the outside world, cocooning calms my sensitive system, releases other people's energies and emotions, and recenters me.

Neutralizing Unnecessary Drama

Life can be very dramatic. For empaths, neutralizing unnecessary drama means not taking on other people's drama, or drama that isn't yours. People you interact with might come across as very dramatic because they are dealing with incredibly stressful, life-threatening, or important issues; they are experiencing dramatic emotions like fear, panic, or despair; they are creating drama in a subconscious bid to get attention because they're lonely; they are becoming used to and comfortable with operating in a fight-flight-freeze mode; they are going through major life transitions; they are experiencing old trauma resurfacing; or they are hoping someone, like you, will mirror their dramatic emotions so they don't have to hold the big emotions they are feeling all by themselves.

At any time, you yourself might fall into one of these categories. Whatever reason people or situations around you seem loaded with drama, remember that the people feeling dramatic are really feeling it. While it might be tempting to try to talk someone out of their emotional experience, or jump in and try to manage it for them, remember that:

- **Other people's emotions are real for them, and therefore valid.** You never know what past trauma a current issue is triggering for someone, or how their emotions feel in their own system and how emotions are experienced by them in general.
- **It's not your job to manage, change, or contain other people's emotions.** You might diplomatically and compassionately suggest that someone get support for their emotions from a doctor or therapist or other resource, but often you cannot force them to do so.
- **As a sensitive person, you are most powerful and safe when anchored in your own emotional experience.**
- **Giving others the freedom to have their own emotional experience gives you the grace to have your own as well.**

Sometimes when you are steeped in a collective energy that is highly dramatic—like living in an area that has experienced an awful tragedy, or working in an office where managers don't typically handle deadlines, pressure, and stress well—you can take on the collective dramatic vibe in your own system. This might also happen if someone close to you is going through something dramatic—like a big career transition or healing journey—and you have been acting as a source of support or comfort.

Signs you might be taking on someone else's individual drama, or a group's collective drama, include:

- Feeling the need to isolate from a very dramatic person or issue in a way that may seem inappropriate or extreme.
- Experiencing an over-the-top reaction to minor stresses, or difficulty putting issues into a larger perspective.
- Feeling an urgency to change the emotional experience of someone who is feeling dramatic, like insisting that they calm down or trying to talk them out of their feelings.
- Finding yourself feeling dramatically different about collective issues and situations than you have historically, and realizing that while you may have genuinely changed your mind, you might also just be mirroring other people's opinions and viewpoints.
- Having trouble connecting to a baseline energy that feels comfortable, relatively calm, and centered.
- Noticing your body reacting in dramatic ways— like hearing yourself talk in a dramatic tone of voice, experiencing tense muscles, or catching a glimpse of yourself in the mirror with a worried, pained, or very intense expression.

Sometimes the best way to balance your energy as a sensitive person is to expose yourself to a different energy. So if you feel overly exposed to drama, you can mindfully expose yourself to a very chill energy. In this way you can use your tendency as an empath to absorb what's around you to your benefit! It can also help you to have more stamina for the dramatic situations, and people feeling dramatic emotions, that will no doubt always be to some degree a part of your world. While the following exercise might not completely stop you from feeling the drama around you, it could greatly turn down the volume on drama.

CREATE CHILL ENERGY

STEP 1: Empaths can be very sensitive to music, as music has an ability to immediately provoke emotions in us. The year I turned eighteen was one of the most dramatic of my life, and I got very into reggae music, which was no coincidence. While reggae has a long tradition of social themes and political activism, it is also known for spiritual themes and having a relaxing effect. There were some Bob Marley and Peter Tosh songs that saved me, reminding me that there was both a higher power and a chill vibe I could connect to any time, as well as an inner strength that could see me through dramatic times. It's why I added a playlist to my mindfulness book *Zen Teen*. What is your chill soundtrack? If there's a lot of drama swirling around you, create a super-chill playlist that's personalized to you. Hard-driving punk or hip-hop might be exactly what makes you feel chill. Or it could be a mix of genres, like world, classical, jazz, country, and pop. Songs you listened to in the past that remind you of good times, or past hard times you survived and thrived through, can also be great additions.

STEP 2: Identify the activities that make you feel chill. Maybe that's physical activities like playing golf, swimming, yoga, or walking? Perhaps you have a creative hobby like knitting, jewelry-making, or coloring that always calms you. Rewatching BBC and *Masterpiece* dramatizations of old novels is very comforting for me—the stories and familiar characters take me out of myself, and because I know how everything resolves I can watch it serenely. Make space for these chill activities in your schedule during dramatic times.

STEP 3: Notice who embodies chill for you. Is it a friend who seems to always take life in stride and put tough issues in perspective? Maybe there is a celebrity, author, spiritual leader, or comedian who always makes you feel more calm. I know someone whose embodiment of chill is Louise Hay, the pioneering self-help author. Whenever this friend is feeling all the dramatic feels, he listens to audio of this author speaking her soothing affirmations. Light Watkins is someone I follow on Instagram, and I enjoy his insights and calm, sincere, grounded energy. Mindfully expose your-self to your chillness gurus. They might be people who seem to handle dramatic times and issues with grace, nurturing, and mindful awareness.

STEP 4: Use any of these techniques not only when others around you are experiencing drama that you might absorb, but also when dealing with your own personal drama and the very dramatic phases of your life.

> **MANTRA**
> Drama will always be part of life. I can balance that energy by mindfully absorbing chill vibes.

Sitting with Uncomfortable Energy

There might be times when empaths say "yes" to something, even though it might put them in an unhealthy, vulnerable, risky position—simply because the empath can sense how much the other person wants them to agree. Saying "no" when you realize a situation may be unnecessarily treacherous or even unsafe, and allowing yourself to be cautious in a healthy way, is absolutely nonnegotiable.

Sometimes the "no" might be temporary, like saying "no" to a certain course of treatment for a minor health issue or elective surgery so you can investigate your other options. Other times the "no" might be firm, like telling your partner "no" when they want to drain your retirement savings by buying something that feels to you like a frivolous indulgence, or telling them "no" when they want to experiment sexually with other people in a way that might put your physical health at risk.

Predators, like scam artists and people with violent tendencies, might be counting on your having weak boundaries around the word "no." Just because you can feel the urgency and desire for you to say "yes" coming from the other person, or a group of people in society, it doesn't mean that others know what's best for you or for a situation. Being able to say "no" and hold to it involves getting used to sitting with uncomfortable energies and emotions.

Years ago, my partner wanted to invest more in one of our current strategies, and I thought we'd invested enough money already and that it was unwise to put more into it. We argued for weeks about it, and at times the energy in our tiny Manhattan apartment was very uncomfortable! I remember telling my therapist about it at the time, and saying, "Maybe I should just give in, do what he wants, and end the standoff so we can enjoy each other's company again."

"That might make you feel better today," my therapist remarked, "but how will you feel months or years from now? What will you look back and think about this moment?"

I realized I would look back and wish I had stood my ground, despite the uncomfortable energy. And in hindsight, in this instance, I turned out to be correct about the investment decision. While my partner makes most of our investment decisions and does an excellent job, years later he told me, "I'm so glad you talked me out of doing that."

Building up your threshold for sitting with uncomfortable emotions and energies is imperative as a sensitive person so that you don't become a people-pleaser. Your life demands that you be able to make decisions that are in your best interest, instead of always going along with what other individuals or the collective herd think is best.

PLAY WITH YOUR THRESHOLD FOR SITTING WITH UNCOMFORTABLE ENERGY

STEP 1: Pick an average week, when you will probably get the opportunity to say "yes" and "no" a lot, like an average work or school week, or a week doing routine activities. If a big issue comes up, like a big relationship, career, financial, or health issue, don't feel the need to include that decision in this experiment. Instead, take your time with those major decisions.

STEP 2: For the next week, practice saying "no" when it's best for you, even if it might create uncomfortable energy. An example is telling a child that no, they cannot put off a chore to another day because company is coming this weekend and you want to ensure a clean home.

STEP 3: During this week, fall back on any healthy emotional or mindfulness coping techniques you use to help you sit with uncomfortable energy—like meditation, talking to someone supportive, cocooning, retreat-and-recover time, or carrying your empath talisman. At the end of the week, notice if your threshold for sitting with uncomfortable energy is greater than when you started, or notice any changes since the beginning of this exercise.

> **MANTRA**
> As a sensitive person, I can get more comfortable with the uncomfortable energy my "no" can create.

Experimenting with Different Levels of Stimulation

While empaths might say "yes" to people-please, they might also say "no" to others simply as a way to protect themselves from possible overstimulation. Sometimes this works as a protection method. If you've had a busy week at work or school during the day plus a busy week of social engagements or personal obligations in the evenings, it might be the perfect protection method to say "no" to anything big on the weekend. A Saturday puttering around the house might be just what your sensitive system requires to recalibrate. Other times, protecting yourself from possible overstimulation could be resisting a nourishing experience.

Recently I was at a small family reunion, where six adults and three children were all spending a long weekend at a rented house. One afternoon while we were sitting and chatting outside, one of the adults suggested we call two family members who weren't able to come to the reunion. "We can just call them right now on speakerphone and all chat! Won't that be fun?"

The sensitive empath in me thought it might actually *not* be fun—there was a lot of stimulation already with all these people in the house, and now we would loop in two more? Plus, would the other relatives feel ambushed that we were calling them cold and putting them on speaker? I felt all the resistance to this idea well up inside me, yet I've learned that when I go with this family member's creative, impulsive ideas, nine times out of ten I'm really glad I said "yes." Sometimes the sensitive side of me can resist doing things spontaneously, without details and schedules nailed down, even in low-stakes, everyday situations like this.

Turns out we all shared a nice, hour-long phone call where everyone caught up and laughed. A hilarious new nickname for my uncle was born on that call, one that I hope sticks through the years. Afterward, I felt very nourished and connected, and I think my relatives who could not come to the reunion felt cared for and included.

While it's important to read the stimulation levels around you and protect yourself from becoming drained and overwhelmed as a sensitive person, there's also value in pushing through and stretching yourself. At times you can hold comfortably more stimulation than you think—just like a human womb can stretch to hold a whole other life. One of the rewards of experimenting with different levels of stimulation might be a greater feeling of engagement with life.

OPEN TO SPONTANEITY

STEP 1: On a week when you feel relatively relaxed, rested, and naturally more open, set the intention to be more spontaneous.

STEP 2: This week, practice saying "yes" to things that may require engagement with a higher level of stimulation than you normally prefer or think you might enjoy. An example might be saying "yes" to a friend when they invite you to do something out of your comfort zone, like attend their weekly improv comedy class, when you two normally share a quiet coffee or lunch date. It could be something big—like saying "yes" to being spontaneously invited to collaborate with someone very successful in your field. Or it could be smaller, like saying "yes" to your partner's request to spontaneously hit the grocery store at peak hours because they're craving making you a special dinner.

STEP 3: As the week goes on, enter situations with an open curiosity. Always feel free to say "no," especially if you're sure you won't enjoy something, become unexpectedly drained or anxious, or you're just enjoying a chill afternoon and don't want to break out of your comfort zone. By the end of the week, hopefully life will have sent you a few—maybe big, maybe small—invitations to safely step out of your comfort zone of stimulation and spontaneously experiment with different levels of stimulation.

> **MANTRA**
> I can develop more stamina for stimulation, and experiment with different levels of stimulation, if the reward is more nourishing experiences with special people.

Equipping Shared Spaces for Sensitivity

In my book *Self-Care for Empaths*, I introduced the value of having an empath sanctuary. This could be a whole room—like a study or bedroom—where you are the primary occupant so you can dial in the vibes just the way an empath might prefer: soft lighting, music, and fabrics. Or a sanctuary can be a temporary space, like turning a shared bathroom into an empath sanctuary for an hour so you can lock the door, soak in the tub, and enjoy a low-stimulation setting—while children, partners, roommates, and animals are in another room! In an empath-sanctuary environment, your sensitive nervous system can settle down and reset.

But what about shared spaces that rarely offer guaranteed privacy, like a shared dorm suite, a kitchen in a house with lots of children, or an open-area office where several desks are in one room? With a few tweaks, these spaces can also be equipped to promote sensitivity. Keep in mind that empaths can be more sensitive to their surroundings because the state of physical surroundings creates a certain energy or vibe. Some general guidelines for shared spaces include:

- **Managing clutter.** Some empaths might be distracted by clutter and mess. In a shared kitchen or bedroom, see if everyone can agree to leave it tidy when not in use, like making the bed in the morning and putting dirty dishes away at night.
- **Keeping noise levels low.** While a roommate or office mate may love loud, pumped-up music, and so might an empath, this will probably grate on an empath sooner. Empaths should all build a shrine to whoever invented headphones and earplugs! Remind yourself and others to use headphones and earbuds responsibly to promote hearing health.
- **Avoiding harsh physical stimuli.** Whether it's a harsh fluorescent light in a boardroom or a harsh smell coming from the bathroom, some empaths are more sensitive to physical stimuli. If you work in an open-area office and coworkers often splurge on delicious but strong-smelling takeout, you might encourage people to get away from their screens and eat lunch in the park, or ask the company to invest in a high-quality indoor air filter to minimize odors.
- **Increasing the cozy quotient.** Anything that makes the physical body feel more at ease, and generally snug,

counts as cozy. When the physical body is comfortable—like snuggling in a nest of plush pillows on a couch—the mind and nervous system can more easily relax. The popularity of weighted blankets proves the calming effect of snugness. Cultivating cozy energy could also be about making a very large space feel smaller and more intimate.

- **Incorporating nature elements.** Whether it's fresh flowers or a cute houseplant, empaths love to match their energy to nature's gentle, stable vibes, which can encourage empaths to "just be." If you'd like to incorporate all four elements, light a candle (and extinguish it safely), get an aromatherapy diffuser, put on some ocean sounds, and place a lovely stone or crystal nearby.

- **Being mindful of aesthetic preferences.** It's amazing how instantly, and positively, people react to a room they find beautiful, or one that matches their personal aesthetic. One person might adore tchotchkes, or knickknacks, while another is a staunch minimalist. Check in with others before purchasing something for the space, to make sure that colors and patterns are pleasing to the collective eye. In my experience with sensitive clients, empaths can be very nourished by beauty, which is subjective.

Compromise with others regarding shared spaces, and remember that you can create a temporary empath sanctuary almost anywhere!

UPDATE A SHARED SPACE WITH EMPATH SANCTUARY VIBES

STEP 1: Locate a space you share with others that you can update with empath sanctuary vibes and make more conducive to sensitivity.

STEP 2: Let others know what you're up to! You can just explain that you want to "cozy up the space" or "keep things more tidy." If it's someone you don't know well, like a new dorm-mate or coworker, no need to go into a long spiel about sensitivity. Do communicate that you want this to be a more inviting place for them too, and get their input.

STEP 3: Consult the list of guidelines above, and discern how you can better manage clutter, keep noise levels low, avoid harsh physical stimuli, increase the cozy quotient, incorporate nature elements, and be mindful of aesthetic preferences. You may be able to knock out two things on this list at the same time, like investing in pretty baskets that will both better manage clutter and beautify the space.

> **MANTRA**
> Making shared spaces more conducive to sensitivity protects my own empath heart while encouraging others to connect with their sensitive side.

Communicating When People in the Present Trigger Wounds from the Past

As an empath, you might be very sensitive to other people's tender spots. While you're with a group of friends, someone excitedly announces that they are pregnant. You might be the one to subtly squeeze the hand of another friend under the table for support, knowing that they tried to get pregnant themselves unsuccessfully years ago and are probably experiencing all the feelings. When you hear that a neighbor has lost someone to cancer, you might be the person on the block who reminds others that this is actually that family's second tragedy of this kind, because decades ago another relative of that same neighbor did not survive cancer. Being attuned to the suffering of others and offering gentle support or simple presence so that others are not alone in their pain is one of the many ways empaths can show up emotionally for others.

We all have old wounds that heal by degrees over time, yet the scars and pain never fully go away. It's comforting when we don't have to always communicate our tender spots to others—they just know. Or with empaths, we just *feel*. Because of your naturally high level of emotional awareness and intuition, you might just feel where the tender spots of others are located.

However, that doesn't mean others will have an intuitive map to your own tender spots and be able to extend the same grace to you. Communicate your tender spots to others proactively, especially when you are flooded with challenging emotions in the present about an old wound from the past. This is great practice for empaths in learning how to prioritize their own needs and emotional experience with themselves and others.

TELL OTHERS WHEN YOU ARE FEELING TENDER

STEP 1: The next time you find yourself having an over-the-top reaction to a minor stressor—like being flooded with anger when your boss asks you to stay an hour late at work one day, or breaking down in tears when a romantic interest asks over text for a rain check on tomorrow's lunch date—discern if this minor stressor from the present is bringing up wounds and intense emotions from the past.

STEP 2: Take a beat to acknowledge to yourself that you are being triggered. This is important. Put your hand over your heart, take a few breaths, or tell yourself something soothing. You're having a painful experience, so show yourself kindness.

STEP 3: Then, in straightforward, simple terms, let the other person know what's going on with you emotionally. Like saying to your boss, "I'm not sure I can stay late this afternoon—I'm really sorry. I know you may not have picked up on it, but I'm still a little fried from staying late so often last month to get through that deadline." The request may have also brought up childhood trauma around not being able to set healthy boundaries for yourself with authority figures, which you don't necessarily have to share with your boss. Only share with others what you're comfortable communicating. Regarding the other example, you might text your romantic interest: "Of course we can do a rain check. I really appreciate your letting me know in advance too because, as I shared with you a while ago, I'm still tender from my last relationship where plans were often canceled last-minute."

STEP 4: Ask yourself how you can apply a new level of healing to this old wound now that it has resurfaced. This is the silver lining of being triggered—with all the challenging emotions comes the invitation to meet the old wound with new medicine. Sometimes simply being more communicative with others about your old wound is healing. Watch for synchronicities, like someone you communicate to recommending a great book on healing childhood abandonment issues or receiving a free gift certificate in the mail for a twenty-minute foot massage after being triggered at work so you can get better at nurturing yourself through triggers.

STEP 5: Getting help for past wounds or lingering PTSD is imperative and can greatly enhance your quality of life. Seeking support from experienced health-care providers can facilitate healing breakthroughs. Find that assistance when you need it.

MANTRA
As a very sensitive person, I may be more sensitive to another person's emotional triggers. When others who are not as sensitive can't give me the same grace, I use that as an excuse to practice communicating my own emotional experience more proactively with others.

Protection Tips for Observing and Witnessing

Let's conclude this chapter on protection with a reminder that one of the best protection tools you can employ as an empath is choosing to sometimes *witness and observe* instead of always *feeling and absorbing*. While it's not a perfect practice, simple awareness of your options can be empowering. This technique gets easier and comes more naturally with time! Keep the following in mind to enter witnessing/observer mode:

- Instead of going into your heart to feel with someone, go into your head to observe.
- Connect with your energy body, which is larger than your physical body. Feel or imagine your energy body— which you can visualize as a garment, a shape, or a color—pulling back into your physical body to create healthy energetic space between you and others.
- Get curious about what the other person might be experiencing emotionally and energetically.
- Name and describe what they might be feeling in your thoughts as you witness them. For example: "My manager seems anxious. It's probably about that big deadline at the end of the week. They usually get stressed this close to a major deadline."
- Consciously ground into your own energy, like by holding your empath talisman, imagining yourself rooted like a tree, or simply taking nice even breaths.
- Keep your body language relaxed and neutral, and keep the tone of your voice calm.
- Engage your claircognizant psychic pathway, focusing on breakthrough thoughts and mental downloads as guidance.
- Once the interaction is over, take your attention immediately to another topic or point of focus.

SENSITIVITY OF AN EMPATH, STRENGTH OF A WARRIOR

Rate yourself on the following warrior principles, as honestly as you can, on a scale from 1 to 4—4 having mastered this warrior trait, 3 being okay at it, 2 being somewhat uncomfortable with it, and 1 representing struggling with this warrior trait most of the time. Keep track of your answers!

1. Like all people with healthy warrior energy, I try to live by a code of honor and treat others as I myself would like to be treated.

2. Being a warrior means being comfortable with stepping outside my comfort zone, but I don't take unnecessary and dangerous risks.

3. My warrior energy helps balance my softer side, so that when I need to be tough with others or to set boundaries, I can.

4. I realize that my warrior strength helps me feel safe being vulnerable with others.

5. As a warrior I'm prepared to—at times when it's healthy and appropriate—sacrifice my individual wants and preferences for the greater good of a relationship or group of people.

6. I relish a healthy challenge and love rising to the occasion!

7. I have a good relationship with self-discipline, so that discipline doesn't feel like a punishment but rather a welcome ally.

8. Being proactive and taking ownership of my life is a warrior trait I had to practice for a while, but now it comes naturally.

9. As a warrior I can seek out and rest in the calm eye of an emotional storm, like when I'm around a group of people experiencing intense emotions and energy.

10. I am resilient, and when I experience a disappointment, I know how to bounce back.

11. While I have been victimized by others, I prefer to think of myself as a survivor.

12. As a sensitive warrior I consider myself on a mission of compassion. Sometimes that means stretching myself to feel compassion for people who may not naturally stir that emotion in me.

13. While I value self-reliance and know how to be my own savior and superhero, I also know when to ask for help and how to value interdependence too.

The above are some core principles of warrior energy, and everyone has an inner warrior! If you scored a 1 or 2 on any warrior trait, simply take it as an invitation to adopt that trait more proactively into your daily life—the warrior inside will enjoy the challenge. Connect with your warrior energy by imagining what your inner warrior looks and acts like. Is it someone from history, pop culture, or a character from your favorite book, television show, or film?

Your inner warrior is a friend to your sensitive empath heart. Your sensitivity and your strength are complementary forces in you: partners. Strength is a foundational element, providing the stability that allows other aspects to flourish, like the trusted spotter who holds a cheerleader aloft so they can flip through the air, or the sturdy figure skater who holds their teammate steady so they can bend expressively and dance across the ice in a more nuanced way. Developing a peace-loving, compassionate inner warrior is an important part of protecting yourself, as well as maximizing the potential and power of your sensitivity.

Chapter 3

Understanding Your Intuitive Heart

As a professional intuitive, one of the most common questions I'm asked is "How can I improve my intuition?" In this chapter, I'll offer tips to make the most of your intuitive ability, like *do* eat healthy and *don't* second-guess your intuitive instincts. But my number-one answer to that question about improving intuition is to learn more about your intuition.

While intuition is a mystical part of your makeup, it's still something that can be understood—to a degree—in a nuts-and-bolts way. Think of your intuition as a first-class engine in a fine automobile. In this chapter we'll be lifting up the hood on your sixth sense and exploring some of the common mechanisms your intuition uses to send you guidance.

As an empath, you are naturally strong in the clairsentience, or the *feeling* psychic pathway. We'll also explore in more depth the other three psychic pathways—clairaudience, or hearing intuitive guidance; clairvoyance, or seeing intuitive guidance, and claircognizance, or knowing intuitive guidance. Discern what other psychic pathways you may have open, and which ones you can play with developing.

There are limits to your intuition, which I cover in more detail in my book *Angel Intuition*. Here we'll be focusing more on your intuitive potential. As someone who uses her intuition to help strangers all over the world navigate life, I can assure you that human intuitive potential can be astounding.

Healing Project or Balanced Relationship?

Often during an intuitive session, a client and I look back on past romantic relationships. Once someone has experienced a bit of hindsight, it's helpful to discern what drew a client to a romantic interest in the first place. It's usually a few factors, and your own intuition can be expert at untangling and identifying those various factors when you can receive guidance about the relationship in witnessing/observer mode.

In my view, people might have, in some cases, soul agreements or contracts to have a relationship with someone else in this lifetime. There can be an invitation for both parties to do some learning or healing through the relationship. And of course there is the invitation to love someone else and be loved in return. With sensitive empath clients, I began discovering another pattern—empaths who were very nurturing or had a strong inner healer would sometimes be intuitively drawn to lovers who were, in part, healing projects. (A fantastic empath expert I follow, Robert Ohotto, shared in an online workshop I attended after I worked on this section of the book that he too has observed this same pattern among empaths.)

A very compassionate empath who loves to support others might be drawn to a romantic partner because the empath can intuitively sense the other person's wounds, and feels compelled to help. Not being consciously aware of this aspect of their attraction (certainly they can also be attracted to other aspects of this person in a healthier way), the empath might believe this strong pull is true love. Rather, it's their inner healer truly wanting to be of service.

The good news is, once an empath who has fallen into this self-sabotaging pattern becomes conscious of it, the pattern can be shifted. This doesn't mean choosing perfect people with no issues—since those "perfect" humans don't exist! It does mean looking for partners who are actively aware of, curious about, and working on their issues, or are at least open to growth, change, and healing.

If you are an empath whose heart goes out to people who are suffering, loves to support others, and finds it easy to be compassionate, ask yourself if you are attracted to a romantic partner because they need you or because you love them. There's a difference. Also, both can be true. Life and love are complex. If you suspect you were partly drawn to a current romantic partner because of their wounds, that doesn't necessarily mean it's an unhealthy partnership or that you should end the relationship.

Over the course of eight years and thousands of intuitive readings, I had so many empath clients with a strong inner healer who fell into this unhealthy pattern that I came up with a piece of advice I share often. If you have a strong inner healer, once you become conscious of that healer inside and mindfully let it have intentional healing projects through your work in the world, it's much easier to keep your inner healer out of your personal relationships.

I've had clients with a strong inner healer who work in the medical community, but also in the entertainment industry, financial industry, and educational system. If you suspect you have a strong inner healer, it doesn't mean you need to drop everything and become a nurse. But finding a way that you can make a meaningful difference in the lives of people who are wounded and suffering, like through volunteer work, might be a gift not only to the world but to yourself. If you're a barista, for example, your inner healer might love to make customers smile or find a way to brighten their day. Letting your inner healer do its thing in a balanced way can be a deeply nourishing experience for you!

It's not just romantic partners who can become healing projects. The friend who only talks about themselves and their issues, expecting constant advice and comfort from you, might be, partially, a healing project. Or the coworker who always asks you to stay late and take on more while they often take off for the afternoon because they are dealing with a lot in their personal life might be a healing project. If you suspect someone in your life is a draining healing project, try shifting the dynamic to see if the relationship can become more balanced and mutually beneficial. While every relationship will go through cycles where one person shows up for the other more, in general you should be giving and receiving, being supported by the other person too.

DIALOGUE WITH YOUR INNER HEALER

STEP 1: Go to a quiet place where you can calm your mind and connect with your intuition. Ask your intuition if someone from your past was partially a healing project. You might hear someone's name in your mind, see an image of someone's face in your mind, have a mental download in thoughts about someone, or you might think of someone and get chills.

STEP 2: Connect to the part of you that is compassionate and nurturing, and that longs not to judge others for their wounds but rather to encourage healing. Ask your inner healer how they are currently fulfilling the urge to encourage healing in others. It might be by pumping up the confidence of an insecure coworker, helping a family who is struggling to finance their first home through your job at a credit union, spending time with a child in your extended family who needs some extra TLC, or volunteering to walk dogs at your local shelter. When your inner healer is engaged in a balanced and appropriate way, helping others feels deeply rewarding. This requires prioritizing your own self-care and having healthy boundaries so you don't slip into burnout.

STEP 3: If you weren't able to identify healthy ways your healer currently gets to come out and offer medicine to the world, ask Archangel Raphael, the healing angel, to provide you with synchronicities about ways you can connect more with your inner healer. Simply say a silent prayer or write Archangel Raphael a quick note in your journal. Then watch for signs about ways you can mindfully engage your inner healer.

MANTRA
There is a part of me that longs to bring medicine to the world. When I connect with my inner healer consciously, my intuition will show me opportunities to support others in balanced, nourishing ways.

Looking at a Relationship from the Spiritual Perspective

One of the most healing things a client and I can do in an intuitive session is to look at a current or past relationship in my client's life from a *spiritual perspective.* I believe spirituality is a very personal concept. You might have grown up Catholic and feel very at-home in that religion. Or you might discover Buddhism and feel that you've found your true path. Pagan traditions may call to you, or your unique spirituality might draw from many sources.

For now, let's define spirituality as something larger than yourself that you feel very much a part of. You could experience this feeling of deep connection when you're walking in nature under an open sky, or when you're resting in Savasana pose during your favorite yoga class, or while you're helping others at a volunteer job.

The spiritual perspective of a relationship could reveal the larger or deeper meaning about why someone wonderful, or someone very challenging, came into your life. Looking for the spiritual perspective involves asking yourself how you (and maybe also the other person) changed, healed, grew, or learned from the relationship. This does not necessarily mean you feel that Spirit brought this person into your life. It can be that you simply want to assign more meaning to the experience, for your own healing, by viewing this relationship through a spiritual lens.

Discerning the spiritual perspective, or perspectives, about a relationship is not intended to bypass your own emotions or experiences. Sensing that a dear old friend came into your life so that as souls you could support each other through this earthly journey is lovely and profound. However, that doesn't mean this friend can't piss you off sometimes, or that you should have no boundaries around them! You could get your dream job, and sense deep down that you were always meant to work at this company with this particular manager, or that you were meant to manage and mentor a particular coworker. Yet there may be a time when it's best to move on and go after a new opportunity, adventure, and relationship. This can happen in long-term romantic partnerships too, when a relationship that was once supportive and felt so aligned or divinely orchestrated hits its expiration date.

If you've had a traumatic or very painful experience with someone, be gentle with yourself as you look at the spiritual perspective. While you might find that it provides you with a comforting silver lining, you might instead find that this strategy just doesn't work or apply with some people you've encountered. It's certainly never meant to justify or excuse someone treating you abusively. The spiritual perspective is also not meant to be interpreted as "everything happens for a reason." When people say that, I think they mean well. Yet there are some chaotic, painful, tragic experiences in life that we make meaningful only by the way we survive or respond to them.

Sometimes a person comes into your life for several reasons—to support and lift you up, perhaps, but also to show you where your boundaries or self-love practice needs some work. This isn't an either/or scenario. And discerning the spiritual perspective doesn't mean you have to forgive someone or invite them back into your life. Was everyone we interacted with meant to come into our life for some deeper reason? I obviously can't say for certain, but I'm guessing the answer is no. Yet I believe some people *were* meant to come into our lives, and the spiritual perspective might help you discern the deeper reasons why.

Because empaths can get pretty emotionally and energetically entangled with others, looking at the spiritual perspective of a relationship takes an empath out of what they're feeling with their extremely developed clairsentient ability, and puts that empath into a more curious, detached, intellectual state. This activates the claircognizant psychic pathway, the domain of intuitive mental downloads and "aha" thoughts and breakthroughs, which we'll work with in the exercise below.

Leaning into the spiritual perspective can be a healthy way for empaths to get energetic and emotional space from others—and even from an empath's own complex emotions. From that more objective place that the spiritual perspective provides, it's easier to get clarity, set boundaries, grow closer, or even let someone leave your life entirely. The spiritual perspective as a tool can help an empath get closure and move on from a relationship that's been over for a long time in practical terms, yet still lingers emotionally—and energetically. In those cases, examining the spiritual perspective may help cauterize a heart wound. Other times, the spiritual perspective might reinforce the significance and sacredness of keeping someone in your life.

ENGAGE YOUR HIGHER SELF

STEP 1: Pick someone you currently have a good relationship with, as well as someone from the past that you had a more challenging relationship with. If you had a very challenging or traumatic relationship with someone, I suggest not using them for this strategy and instead working with a professional counselor.

STEP 2: Get out your journal and put on some relaxing ambient music or nature sounds.

STEP 3: Since empaths are incredibly intuitive, use your intuition to discern the deeper wisdom around why someone came into your life. Instead of being in your heart with your feeling *clairsentient* intuitive ability, go into your head to engage your *claircognizant* psychic pathway. Activate this pathway by quieting your mind and getting *curious*. Keep your mind as blank as you can while you ponder the following questions, waiting for out-of-the-box intuitive insights to pop into your mind as fully formed thoughts or downloads.

STEP 4: Start with the person you currently have a good relationship with. Ask your soul, higher self, or wise self what the larger reason is that this person came into your life. Your higher self's wisdom is the wisdom of detachment. Claircognizance also operates best when you are detached in a healthy way. The higher self can take more into account—like your highest good and also the highest good of others. Your higher self has access to the larger map of your life, so it can see the forest for the trees.

STEP 5: Now ask your higher self how you and the other person have changed, healed, grown, or learned from the relationship. What insights are you experiencing? Write them down in your journal.

STEP 6: Repeat steps 4 and 5, concentrating on the person with whom you have a challenging relationship.

> ### MANTRA
> Looking at the spiritual perspective engages my intellectual psychic pathway and the higher self's wisdom of detachment. My emotional experiences with someone are a different kind of wisdom–and equally important to acknowledge, process, express, and consider.

Using Synchronicity as a Second Opinion on Your Own Intuition

You probably expect someone like me to tell you "Trust your intuition!" And it's true: what often derails our own intuitive ability is a lack of faith in our sixth sense. When you don't trust and value your intuition, you could have an accurate and powerful gut instinct or "aha" realization about someone in your life—yet not follow your own guidance because you second-guess your intuition. Days, weeks, or months later you might look back and think, "Oh, I had an intuitive hit about this! I wish I had listened and acted on it."

However, your intuition isn't foolproof. You can want a relationship to turn out one way so much that you confuse your own will and desire with genuine intuitive guidance. Or you might be feeling so emotional that it's difficult to calm down and connect with your intuition. That's why when you're considering a big issue in a relationship—like whether to commit to someone, get out of a business contract with someone, or invest in a property with someone—it's always wise to get a second opinion on your own intuitive hunches. This might look like consulting a colleague with great intuitive instincts, or calling a good friend who is objective about the situation and very sensitive, or even contacting a professional intuitive like me.

My favorite way to get a second opinion on my own intuition is through synchronicity. A synchronicity or sign from the universe is a meaningful coincidence. Like needing to find a specialist doctor and going to a dinner party where one of the other guests happens to know a doctor specializing in your issue. Or having a fight with a family member and then watching a movie to relax, only to realize that the movie you "randomly" chose has themes that help you see the situation with your loved one in a new, healing light.

Synchronicities can happen organically, or you can call them in, which we'll practice in the next exercise. When trying to discern if something that happened to you was a synchronicity, consider the following:

- Did the moment feel heavy with meaning and dense, heightened, or electric energetically?
- Did time seem to slow down and you felt more present in the moment?
- When the synchronicity happened, or when you thought about it afterward, did you experience any physical intuitive sensations, like getting chills all over?
- Has the experience naturally come back to mind, or stuck out in your memory, days or weeks afterward?
- Was the synchronicity timed well, like advice that was exactly what you needed to hear exactly *when* you needed to hear it? Or being contacted by someone right after you were thinking about them? Or having an offer of work come in right when you needed extra cash?
- Did you receive repetitive synchronicities about the same issue, like seeing an ad for a book that interests you, then the next week reading a helpful article by an expert and

realizing afterward that this was the author of the same
book, and then the next week having a friend recommend
that same book to you "randomly"?

▨ Did the synchronicity seem remarkable, like something
happening unexpectedly or in an extraordinary manner?

Your intuition works best when you remain open and curious. So be
open about getting a synchronicity, and curious about whether it confirms,
informs, or challenges your own intuitive hits.

JOURNAL TO CALL IN SYNCHRONICITIES

STEP 1: Get out your journal and open it to a blank page. At the top of
the page, address your journal entry to the divine in any way that resonates with you: Dear Spirit, Dear Angels, Dear Universe, Dear God, Dear
Goddess, Dear Life.

STEP 2: Spend a few sentences writing about something you're grateful for. It could be something big and exceptional like a recent relationship milestone, career achievement, or financial win. Or it could be
something that seems smaller but is actually huge—like feeling grateful for shelter or food. Or you might express gratitude for something
ordinary that has an extraordinarily positive impact on your day, like
your morning pick-me-up drink, the pet who loves to snuggle, or the
view of your backyard garden. You are trying to attract a synchronicity, and gratitude is a very attractive energy! Pick something that
creates an authentic energy of gratitude within you to help manifest
this synchronicity.

STEP 3: Now ask for a synchronicity as guidance about an issue in your
life. You might need a synchronicity about which job offer to take, who
to go on vacation with, or how to handle an intimacy issue with your

partner. Remember not to put any conditions on the synchronicity . . .
like when or where it will appear, or what form it will take.

STEP 4: Write a brief line of thanks in your journal, and put it away. For
the next few days, be on the lookout for synchronicities regarding this
issue. Consult the guidelines in this section to help discern if something
is a synchronicity.

STEP 5: Remember that your intuition and synchronicities are just one
element of decision-making. Be sure to check in with your emotional
heart and your practical head, and to get advice from experts—like a
financial planner or medical doctor—as well!

> **MANTRA**
> The more I get used to recognizing synchronicities
> or helpful signs from the universe, the more they
> will appear.

Integrating the Four Clairs or Primary Psychic Pathways

We've already touched on the four primary psychic pathways, the four clairs—
clairaudience (hearing), claircognizance (knowing), clairsentience (feeling),
and clairvoyance (seeing)—which are the foundation of your *internal* intuitive system. When someone identifies as a *clairvoyant* or *clairsentient*, they
are probably naming their dominant psychic pathway. My naturally strongest psychic pathway is clairaudience, or hearing intuitive guidance as a calm,
gentle voice in my mind. As an empath, you may find that clairsentience,
or feeling intuitive guidance as energy, gut instincts, physical sensations, or
another person's emotions in your own system is your dominant clair. For me,
and many others, clairsentience is just one of the clairs I employ to navigate

the world intuitively, as I use all four clairs in my personal life and in sessions with clients. So you might call me a "multi-clair," and I bet you are too.

Get the most out of your intuitive system by identifying different intuitive pathways in yourself, and then integrating them. For instance, in a session with a client, I am hearing guidance as a voice in my mind, seeing images in my mind (while my physical eyes are open), getting intuitive mental downloads, and feeling physical sensations and energy. After eight-plus years of doing intuitive readings on thousands of clients from all over the world, this integration of the clairs happens in a session seamlessly, without effort, and feels very natural. Clairs perform together well, like different instruments in the same orchestra or individual dancers in a ballet. Integration will happen organically the more you are aware of, value, and use your intuition.

Intuition and sensitivity exist on a spectrum. As a professional intuitive who uses her intuition every day with clients and has all four clairs active and open, I would consider myself naturally highly intuitive. Yet my intuition has grown by leaps and bounds with two simple tools: study, and practice. A cabinet-maker masters their craft by learning technique and working every day, and an intuitive like me is the same. Getting better at using your intuition is just like anything else you have worked on, and improved at, slowly over time.

I once heard a very famous professional basketball player admit that the first time he went to basketball camp as a kid, he was absolutely the worst player there! Despite feeling crushed, he used the experience as inspiration, learning all he could about the game and practicing every day. Obviously this young man was naturally talented at athletics, even if he didn't yet realize it; but with knowledge and determination, he became one of the best players in the world. You might consider yourself only moderately intuitive before you read this book; yet after learning about your intuition and relying on it more in everyday situations, you might also come to consider yourself highly intuitive.

If you already have a healthy relationship with your intuition and know a lot about the subject, use this section as a nudge to play with clairs that are not currently open for you—or not as developed. Keep in mind that you can go through sensitivity growth spurts, periods when your sensitivity significantly increases, or a new psychic pathway opens or becomes stronger (we'll explore this in the next section). While I'd had isolated instances of psychic ability as a child and teen, my intuition blossomed in my late twenties, when clairaudience and clairsentience became a regular part of my life. Interestingly, my physical body became more sensitive too, and I had to clean up my diet, be more mindful about taking supplements, and avoid too many chemicals and food additives. Over the next few years, I read everything I could about intuition. During that time, clairvoyance, which I had experienced as eerily accurate intuitive visions in my mind in my early teens, came back fully for me. And I began to understand that breakthrough thoughts and mental downloads I had were actually intuitive and coming from the claircognizant psychic pathway—I'm guessing you get those claircognizant "aha" realizations too!

Everyone's intuition is unique. Mine blossomed during my first Saturn return, a time in life when, according to astrology, you start to get a better idea of what your calling and destiny will be. When did yours blossom? Thirty years ago, last week, or perhaps some point in the future? You might find that clairsentience and claircognizance are intuitive pathways you can access and hone, yet clairvoyance and clairaudience aren't part of your intuitive wiring. It may be true that one person can have clairvoyance as part of their natural intuitive wiring and the pathway is simply dormant, waiting to be activated and explored; while another person may never see mental images in their mind when they are awake, yet they regularly experience intuitive dreams. Intuitive dreams are different from clairvoyance, but they can be just as powerful and helpful as waking mental images.

Part of trusting your intuition is trusting that your unique intuitive makeup is yours for a reason. This is vital! Undervaluing your unique intuitive wiring is undervaluing yourself and all you have to offer—thus your intuition will underperform and the rest of us will not benefit from your unique gifts. Trust your intuition's timing if increased sensitivity occurs or a new psychic pathway opens. Your individual intuition is powerful and everything you need to navigate your unique destiny.

Sometimes intuition can be genetic, and it's fun to see if anyone in your family is also very intuitive. I discovered by accident that one of my relatives is also very intuitive when she described being able to accurately "guess" numbers—like which number would be a lucky number in a raffle—by seeing the number as an image in her mind. Do you have any loved ones who are also sensitive, or able to feel and easily pick up on the energies and emotions around them as well as being more sensitive to physical stimuli? Remember that sensitivity can be influenced and opened up by your environment, so an adopted parent or in-law who is very sensitive and spent a lot of time with you may have helped engage your own sensitivity.

For quick reference:

Clairaudience is *hearing* intuitive information in your mind as a voice. This is different than a thought, and different than hearing with your physical ears. Clairaudience sounds like someone speaking calmly in your head. Clairaudience could be one word, like hearing "left" in your mind when you are wondering which direction to take, or whole sentences, like hearing "He feels the same" when wondering if your partner is also nervous about an upcoming event. In my experience, clairaudience is the rarest psychic pathway to have open. This is different than the voices people with some mental health conditions or severe vitamin and mineral deficiencies or hormone imbalances might hear. The voice will never be loud, menacing, or annoying, and it has a consistent, comforting sound. If you're hearing a voice that is disturbing, investigate with a trusted healthcare provider. If the cause does not seem to be physical or psychological, explore, with a professional intuitive, ways you can better tune into your clairaudience and tune out other random frequencies.

Clairsentience is *feeling* intuitive information, like feeling the collective energy of a group of people at a party, sensing energy of spaces when you walk into a room, or feeling the energy of an individual as intense, neutral, or mild. Empaths will often be able to describe how energy—which cannot be seen—feels, like saying the energy feels light, heavy, calm, electric, or thick. Empaths strong in clairsentience can feel other people's joy or sadness as if it were the empath's own, and may be able to feel physical symptoms of others, like having your knees briefly ache when you call a friend recovering from knee surgery. Physical sensations like chills, or the hair on your arms or the back of your neck standing up, tell an empath when their intuition wants them to pay special attention to something, like getting chills when you hear someone's name or read a piece of information in a book. Did you just get chills? Empath humor!

Claircognizance is *knowing* intuitive information as breakthrough thoughts and mental downloads. Ever have a thought just pop into your head out of the blue, a thought that was new information and out-of-the-box thinking, encouraging you to look at a situation in a different way? That's claircognizance, and it's different than the part of your mind that strategizes its way to answers—also very useful! Claircognizant thoughts pop into your mind fully formed and get your attention (it's not the same old thoughts and worries that cycle around your brain over and over like laundry in a dryer). Intuitive thoughts can come in as a download, where you seem to "know" all about someone else—like their patterns and personality—almost instantly, just like how computers can quickly download large amounts of software.

Clairvoyance is *seeing* intuitive information as images in your mind's eye. Some sensitive people may see auras, ghosts, or other images with their physical eyes, but clairvoyance mainly governs the mind's eye, where images play out on the big screen of your brain whether your physical eyes are open or shut. While clairvoyance is a rarer psychic pathway to have open and active, it's one you can play with opening up (this is less true of clairaudience). As a child, I played with opening up clairvoyance in a game with my brother, and did so with astounding success! My brother would turn away from me and pick different colored cards, one at a time, and I would guess which card he was holding with my eyes closed, allowing the correct color to come into my mind each time. Clairvoyant images can be straightforward, like seeing a mental image of a pink tulip when trying to decide what type of flowers to plant; or they can be symbolic, like seeing an image of someone literally dragging their feet across the ground, or shaking with fear, when wondering if a lover is ready for commitment.

Empaths are naturally strong in the clairsentient or feeling psychic pathway. When people use the term *empath* or *sensitive*, they are usually referring to clairsentience. In the next exercise, we'll play with discerning what other psychic pathways you may have open or be able to access.

PLAY WITH THE FOUR CLAIRS

STEP 1: Identify a clair or clairs you already have open and active—hearing, seeing, knowing, or feeling intuitive guidance.

STEP 2: Identify a clair that is less dominant and developed, or one that doesn't seem to be currently open and active. If you can't decide which one to try, use your intuition to decide! If you *hear* the number "4" in your mind, *see* the number "4" in your mind, or get a strong feeling about the fourth entry when you scan the four clairs in the previous section, that means you should play with clairvoyance.

STEP 3: For at least a week, play with this less dominant or dormant clair.

> For **clairaudience**, if you don't hear a voice in your mind, pay attention to snippets of overheard conversation in the grocery line that stay with you, or a stray sentence of dialogue in a movie that strikes you as having special meaning for you. This is *different* from clairaudience (as clairaudience is a voice in your mind, not your physical ears), but you are still getting used to hearing words as intuitive guidance.

> For **claircognizance**, practice pruning the thoughts in your mind. When you can get better at calming your mind during ordinary moments each day—like while cleaning, shopping, exercising, or reading—it makes room in your mind for those more profound intuitive thoughts to pop in. Practice having a quieter mind with more open space between thoughts.

> For **clairsentience**, let's assume that as an empath you already have a fairly open and developed

clairsentient pathway, so for this exercise I'd encourage you to choose one of the other three. However, if your intuition was drawn to this clair to play with, or being sensitive is a newer experience for you, for one week practice tuning into the energy of spaces, like how you feel or what energy you pick up when you first walk into a restaurant, office space, shop, or yoga studio. Also walk through your home, and see what kind of energy you sense in each room, or in different parts of a big room, or notice how the energy changes with different people there or subtle physical differences like an absence of clutter or the addition of natural light.

■ For **clairvoyance**, find a guided meditation you like online, or sit comfortably with nature sounds or a gentle sound machine playing, and close your eyes. Ask your intuition for some images! Try to keep your mind relaxed and open, not forcing images, but rather noticing what appears. Have fun, and don't try to make sense of the images until you are done meditating. In time, you may be able to see images in your mind's eye with your physical eyes open.

MANTRA
As an empath, my clairsentient, feeling psychic pathway is one of my intuitive assets. Yet my unique intuitive wiring might contain within it the ability to also see, hear, or know intuitive guidance. I'm learning to value and celebrate my own unique intuitive makeup, and view how I experience my intuition right now as powerful.

Navigating Relationships During a
Sensitivity Growth Spurt

People come to me to get my intuitive take on all aspects of their lives, yet occasionally I get a client who comes to me mainly to help them navigate a sensitivity growth spurt. I'm actually surprised it doesn't happen more often, as sensitivity growth spurts are a very real thing, when your intuition and sensitivity suddenly increase and become stronger.

A couple of factors might trigger a sensitivity growth spurt:

- Your system might temporarily experience an increase in sensitivity and intuition to help you navigate a big life transition, and then the increased sensitivity stays with you to a degree.

- You may have changed your diet, gotten sober, increased your self-care, or made some other healthy adjustment to your daily physical routine so that you are no longer numbing out your sensitivity.

- You may have started learning more about intuition and sensitivity, and this awakened something in you or brought your sensitivity more online. Just being around someone a lot who is very sensitive and open about it could do this.

- You might have decreased the amount of stimulation in your life, like getting a job where you are allowed to work from home instead of in a bustling office, or had your twin children suddenly move away to go to college so that your house is much quieter. After the 2020 pandemic. when many people were at home more, several new and previous clients came to me, feeling that their sensitivity had exploded during that time.

- You may have just organically experienced an increase in sensitivity that is hard to pinpoint a reason for, like when a plant that has never blossomed suddenly begins producing beautiful blooms.

Just like you had physical growth spurts as a kid where you suddenly grew a few inches and the pants that fit a few months ago are now too short or your shoes don't fit six weeks after you bought them, you can also have times in life when your intuition grows by leaps and bounds. This *should* be good news, as many people who are naturally sensitive and intuitive are looking to maximize and enhance this ability!

However, when a sensitivity growth spurt happens, it can be disorienting, awkward, or unsettling—just like the initial stages of a physical growth spurt (puberty comes to mind). Think of how superheroes in comic books and movies feel when they first discover their superpowers. It can be a frustrating, even anxiety-producing transition time while they learn what they are capable of and how to manage their new abilities.

Some advice if you are experiencing a sudden, significant increase in sensitivity and intuition:

- **Don't panic!** This is actually quite normal—for those who are wired for high sensitivity. Read books by intuition or sensitivity experts to help normalize what's happening to you. Books on intuition and sensitivity, like this one, or gentle and encouraging books with real-life stories about psychic phenomena, like those by Laura Lynne Jackson and Sonia Choquette or *Angels in My Hair* by Lorna Byrne, can be an affordable and invaluable investment. That alone may help you significantly.
- **Create open space in your schedule.** Part of learning how to manage your new level of sensitivity is simply getting used to it. If your schedule is jam-packed with work and personal engagements, clear empty space on your calendar where you can do some classic retreat-and-recover activities so you have less stimulation to process. This will give you more space to adjust to the increased stimulation of increased intuition and sensitivity, as well as to connect with and get to know this slightly new version of yourself.

- **Find a mentor.** This does not have to necessarily be someone you pay, although it can be. Lots of seasoned professional intuitives like Colette Baron-Reid or Radleigh Valentine, as well as psychology experts like Dr. Judith Orloff, post regular free content that can help. There are also lots of online workshops, podcasts, and memberships produced by sensitive people who have been living, loving, and working with sensitivity for a long time and have much wisdom to share.

- **Talk to a sensitive friend.** Having relationships with other empaths and people who identify as sensitive can be nourishing in general, as you can share sensitivity tips and tools, normalize your experience, and compare what works best for each of you. During a sensitivity growth spurt, relationships with other sensitives can be something to lean into. It could be a large group like an online membership or social-media community, but it can also just be one coworker, friend, or relative you can talk to in an open, safe, supportive way about what's going on with you.

- **Let the people in your life know you need space, support, and gentle energy now.** Anything positive happening can still be overwhelming—simply because it's a change. Sensitivity growth spurts fall into this category. If roommates, partners, and family members are well informed and sympathetic about sensitivity and intuition, let them know you just need to be treated gently for a bit—like avoiding extra stress, drama, stimulation, and harsh energy. That's because it might be easy for you to become frazzled while you get used to this new level of heightened sensitivity. If they aren't as familiar with sensitivity or don't believe in the sixth sense, simply tell others you are just feeling a little more vulnerable and tired lately, and you could use some soft landings. Not everyone in your life has to completely get the whole empath thing. They just need to be generally supportive of you and whatever you need.

- **Ground in the physical world.** Ironically, what always helps anchor your mystical abilities is grounding into the physical world. Develop a healthy and comfortable routine for your days, eat regularly, and get enough sleep. Your sensitivity affects your nervous system, so any healthy grounding activities that fall under the category of good self-care will stabilize your energy and nervous system so you don't go into fight-flight-freeze or overstress your adrenals. Then you can maintain this new level of sensitivity more comfortably and effortlessly.

You will hit a comfortable "new normal" at some point during your sensitivity growth spurt. It could take a few weeks, or it could take a few months. But your system and psyche will adjust—just like when you first learned to ride a bike, swim, speak a different language, read, or drive a car. What once felt new, foreign, and intimidating begins to feel natural and flowing with time and patience.

Be sure to reach out for support along the way, to loved ones, experts, or health-care providers. If things are not settling down in a reasonable amount of time, or you are ever having trouble coping, *definitely* you should reach out so you can get all the support you need. This can be a good time to get a physical checkup with your doctor, or a mental-health checkup with a counselor, just to make sure nothing besides your sensitivity growth spurt is affecting you. Sometimes the hardest, scariest part is admitting that you need help and then taking that first step toward getting it. Remember that as you reach out, the universe will be there to meet you with the help you require. As you reach out for new tools to help manage and understand this sensitivity growth spurt, you might be surprised at how many nourishing new relationships you make and attract in the process—that's always how it's happened for me during sensitivity growth spurts!

IDENTIFY YOUR TOP THREE COMFORTING COPING SKILLS

STEP 1: Some of the coping skills you will need for managing your sensitivity growth spurt will be the same coping skills you use to comfort yourself during any transition that could, at times, be overwhelming. When you think of it that way, you won't feel so lost about how to support yourself!

STEP 2: Reflect on healthy coping skills you have used in the past to help comfort yourself while you navigated transitions, like a career, health, or relationship transition. These might include: talking to a counselor; leaning into your most supportive friendships; taking long baths; taking long walks; getting lost in a great story like a series of novels or a show with a few seasons; spending time with pets or small children; reading or watching feel-good news stories or memoirs/documentaries; making an appointment with an intuitive, acupuncturist, massage therapist, or energy worker; checking in with your doctor, naturopath, or nutritionist; eating healthy and taking your daily supplements or medications; not biting off more than you can chew at work or home; avoiding unnecessary stress and drama; listening to your favorite musical artist or genre of music; feeling connected in nourishing ways like being of service at work, volunteering, or with loved ones; developing a regular journal or meditation practice; getting lost in a creative hobby like playing an instrument, crafting, or cooking; spending time outside in nature like gardening or just chilling in a safe local park; snuggling up with pillows or blankets.

STEP 3: All of the coping skills listed above are ones that seem to help many empaths. Identify at least three that you can incorporate into your daily routine during your sensitivity growth spurt to help you feel more comforted. Remember that because sensitivity growth spurts can at times feel overwhelming, you don't want to further overwhelm yourself by trying to incorporate too many things into your routine. Relaxation and stress relief are part of your goal!

Not Being Talked Out of Your Own Gut Instincts

While you might hear the phrase "gut instinct" used in a general way to describe intuitive guidance, by this point in the book you can probably guess that this is merely one type of intuitive guidance—and a powerful one! Gut instincts are a strong feeling and deep knowing. This is somewhat different than the detached, intellectual knowing of most claircognizance. Gut instincts are a knowing you *feel*, in an immediate, primal, visceral way.

You might have experienced a gut instinct that you should accept a certain job—even if on paper you weren't too sure about it. Or you might have a gut instinct that a family vacation should happen in a certain location—even though you're presented with four very attractive options by other family members. Or you might get a strong gut instinct that the house you're considering buying just isn't the right fit for you.

While gut instincts could be classified as the most simple and straightforward form of intuitive guidance, they can be complicated in the sense that they may at times ask you to go against conventional thinking or the wishes of others. If your gut instinct about something, someplace, or someone stays consistent, pay special attention! Gut instincts can be the deciding factor in many major decisions, especially if you have also taken into account important practical considerations like the opinion of experts, empirical data, the counsel of trusted friends and loved ones, and how your decision will impact others.

If gut instincts are so vital, why is it that humans often look back on decisions from the past and remark, in frustration, "I should have listened to my gut"? The simple answer is that some people don't understand or value their intuition. And even pros like me can at times discount their own gut instincts! As an empath with a naturally strong intuition, you may genuinely value your gut instincts. Where an empath often gets tripped up is not in second-guessing their gut instincts, but in letting others talk them out of their gut instincts. There are simple reasons for this, like:

- When your gut instinct does not match what the other person wants or believes is best, and you people-please to avoid absorbing their displeasure. As an empath you might have to feel the challenging emotions that following your gut instinct will create in others. Therefore, you may choose to avoid that unpleasant absorption, ignore your gut instinct, and go along with an option that is more palatable to others—yet maybe not best for them or you.

  Example: Your gut is telling you to make a career change, but your spouse doesn't like change or uncertainty and wants you to stay at your old job because, to them, it seems like a safer bet. Instead of even compromising, so you both feel comfortable, you just go along with what your spouse wants because it seems easier in the moment emotionally for you as a sensitive person—although, in the long run, this could take a much bigger toll on you emotionally by creating your own challenging emotions.

- When you sense that someone else feels that they need you to say "yes" to them, their project, their dream, etc., but your gut instinct is telling you to say "no." As an empath, you may be able to feel so intimately in your own system how much someone desperately wants you to agree to something that you say "yes"—to avoid sitting in the very uncomfortable energy a "no" can create. This is actually an old-school, and unfortunately successful, sales tactic!

Example: You've been dating someone for a few months, and from the beginning it didn't seem like the best match. Now, two months in, your gut is telling you it would be kindest, to both of you, to end things before the relationship gets serious. Yet you can feel the other person's strong need to partner and intense desire to have you remain in their life. It's overwhelming emotionally to imagine how they would react if you listen to your gut instinct, so you put off the inevitable drama and stay in the relationship a bit longer. Meanwhile, the problem gets worse.

So, how can empaths better honor their gut instincts? Try these tips:

- **Remember to stay in witnessing/observer mode** with others when sharing your gut instincts. Get out of your feeling psychic pathway where you can easily mingle with the energy and emotions of others, and go into your more clinical, detached, intellectual psychic pathway.

- **Engage your higher self** by imagining yourself sitting alone, serenely, high on a beautiful mountain. You're feeling calm and secure. Down below you can witness the world and this issue, but you are observing from a great distance.

- **Write down your gut instinct statement** on a sticky note, in your journal, or somewhere you can keep and reference it. Use brief, simple terms: "I have a hunch that I should not accept this school's college admissions offer" or "Attending this weekend workshop with my good friend feels like an important investment." If your gut instinct stays consistent, then you can consult this gut-instinct statement to empower and motivate yourself. Remember that you're not alone. Your higher self helped you craft that statement and has your back!

- **Consider that your gut instinct might be what's best for others**, even if they can't see it yet. Years from now, with hindsight, a partner may thank you for your decision and validate your gut instinct, even though at the time they strongly disagreed. Also, practice doing what's best for you, even if it's not what others want or need, while being as compassionate, considerate, and diplomatic as possible.
- **Remind yourself that intuition isn't foolproof, and life is organic,** so circumstances and people are always shifting. Give yourself space and permission to review, question, reconsider, or revise your gut instincts—and to receive fresh, new intuitive insights.

Bottom line: Stay connected to your gut instinct—how it feels and how it compels you to act.

BE MORE MINDFUL OF YOUR GUT HEALTH

The gut is often referred to as the "second brain," since the brain and gut are extensively connected by hormones, neurons, and chemical reactions. Taking care of your gut health may help stabilize your nervous system and mood, and when you're feeling calm and grounded it's easier to connect with your intuition and gut instincts.

STEP 1: Set the intention that you'd like to be mindful of your gut health, if it's not something you normally consider.

STEP 2: Observe your gut. Do you sometimes experience indigestion, burping, bloating, excessive gas, nausea, constipation, loose stool, pain, diarrhea, or an acidic stomach? Reach out for expert advice, either in a book about gut health, articles by experts online, or preferably with a health-care provider.

STEP 3: Consider taking some gut-healthy action steps. This could include: taking a probiotic supplement, eating prebiotic foods, getting more fiber in your diet or with supplementation, avoiding sugar, avoiding alcohol and caffeine, trying the elimination diet, getting tested for food allergies, eating a low-glycemic diet, drinking gentle detoxifying teas like ginger or peppermint, or reducing the stress in your life.

Always do your own research and speak to your health-care provider before trying a new supplement, medication, or diet. And remember that you can often make changes slowly and gradually, giving your body time to adjust.

> ## MANTRA
> My gut instincts are a crucial part of my intuitive GPS system, helping me navigate life. While I remain open, flexible, and curious regarding my intuition, I honor my own gut instincts and take good care of my physical gut.

Evaluating Baseline Energy in Yourself & Others

Perhaps the greatest gift you can offer a loved one is allowing them to be themselves. Just as you're hoping others will respect and make allowances for your sensitivity, understanding the baseline energy of a loved one or long-time coworker can help you better respect and make allowances for them.

People's energy really can change temporarily or evolve permanently, both over time naturally and because of circumstances. You've probably watched loved ones become more intense, displaying a high energy, because they are taking better physical care of themselves and have more energy, or perhaps because they are under more stress and the adrenaline is pumping. You surely have seen folks in your life become more chill, or display a milder energy due to various factors, as well as witnessing people suddenly finding it easier to idle into neutral and display a consistent even-keeled energy.

Let's delve into baseline energy, so how someone in your life has most frequently presented over time. I'll break it down, for simplicity's sake, into three main types of energy:

- **Mild:** A sleepier energy that can be very comforting, mild energy is like a cat curling up on a windowsill to sun themselves. Mild energy is soft in a lovely way, and people who may naturally idle at this energy are great at creating a low-stimulation vibe to take the edge off. Think of a gentle hug, a quiet walk on a secluded beach, or your favorite yummy warm drink on a chilly afternoon. One might describe a person with natural mild energy as chill or calm.

- **Neutral:** This energy is like a harp string that's still, waiting to be plucked. While people with neutral energy can get carried along by either mild or intense energy, they idle at a place in the middle of those two. This is an adaptable energy, and people with a naturally neutral energy might find it easier to witness and observe life as well as have a tolerance or appreciation for different energies. Think of neutral energy as the consistent dorm-mate who rises at the same time every day and always makes their bed. During times of emotional storms, they are able to stay "level-headed." This can be a wonderfully stabilizing, grounding, dependable energy for others to vibe off.

- **Intense:** Fireworks, belly laughs, and feeling all the feels—people with intense energy wake life up! Intense energy can be delightful and refreshing. People with naturally intense energy might feel as if they have excess energy, which is why donating some of that energy to other people's projects and visions is such a gift. Intense energy can be extremely motivating and inspiring to others, and people with this energy help others by modeling connection with life in a very immediate, visceral way.

I believe life works best ideally with a balance of all these energies, and that people are made the way they are for a reason—it's part of their unique genius. As someone with a naturally neutral energy, I deeply value having people with more mild and intense energy in my life. I've learned so much from their innate wisdom, and their energy helps balance and inform mine—and offer perspective. At times I also display a more mild or intense energy, so be flexible with these concepts when applying them to yourself and others.

Recognizing your own baseline energy and that of others can help you better navigate energy. You might have days where you're craving more mild, neutral, or intense energy, and knowing this—as well as knowing the people in your life—helps you discern where to get that missing energy. Places can have a baseline energy—like the mild energy of your favorite bookstore. And music can have a predominant energy—like the intense energy of your favorite pop song that makes you want to dance.

Letting other people be themselves and live out their own natural brilliance is a gift to them, and to the world. While you or someone else might feel they have a natural baseline energy, this doesn't mean people should suffer because of it. If you're experiencing intense highs or intense lows or the monotonous doldrums—or in any other way unsatisfied or uncomfortable with your energy—reach out for help. That help could be from a medical professional, another caring human, or any other place that does the trick.

Certain activities might promote mild, neutral, or intense energy—like the neutral energy of date night that begins at your favorite local restaurant, followed by watching a thoughtful or humorous movie with themes you can discuss with your partner before bed. Seeking out energy-specific activities if you're wanting an energy adjustment might help a lot.

IDENTIFY A LOVED ONE'S BASELINE ENERGY

STEP 1: Use your intuition to pick someone to focus on for this exercise and grab a journal or something to write on. Pick someone you've known for several years by quieting your mind—do you see someone's face in your mind, hear someone's name, or have a brilliant thought about someone? If not, think of people who are most important to you, and feel into who you're most drawn to focus on for this exercise.

STEP 2: Does this person display a baseline energy? While all individuals in some ways defy category, you may find that this person fits nicely into one of these three energy categories. You may have even thought of them while reading about this category in the previous section. Or is their energy very mutable? If they don't seem to fit one of the three categories, or if they are a combination of them, describe their energy in your own terms in your journal.

STEP 3: Have you seen this person go through energy shifts that were temporary? Over the years, have you seen their energy evolve or even change categories in a significant way? Jot down your observations.

STEP 4: How does this person's baseline energy complement yours? In what ways is their energy challenging for you? How do you mindfully enjoy the times when your energies jell; and how do you navigate or cope with difficulties or clashes? How does their energy inspire or positively inform your own? Write your answers down for more clarity.

> ### MANTRA
> Understanding the baseline energy of people in my life improves my relationships and helps me better understand my own energy.

Receiving Intuitive Insight about Someone Else

Obtaining intuitive information about someone else—either to help you better understand that person, or to share with that person so they can better navigate their life—is pretty exciting to most sensitive people. As an empath who understands the reality of intuition and its power, it should be exciting! This is something I've done for a living for years with clients, sharing my intuitive insights about their lives and issues.

What's useful when you want to mindfully tune in to someone else for intuitive insight?

- **Being open to your intuitive hits.** The best intuitive hits, or insights, will surprise you! You may be tuning in to a business colleague who's suddenly being prickly and rude with you, trying to discern a reason for this new behavior. When you get the intuitive hit that this person is secretly "threatened by" or "romantically attracted to" you, don't reject the insight just because it's shocking or does not make logical sense if, say, they are more professionally successful than you on paper and claim to be in a happy, committed relationship.

- **Knowing that intuition will pick up on many threads.** When trying to discern someone's motivation for doing something, for example, like a loved one offering to loan you money to pay for a big-ticket house renovation, your intuition will pick up on many threads of motivation. The person might be in a great place financially and, feeling blessed, was already looking for a way to help others when they learned of your predicament. Another thread might be that they are hoping that this strengthens their bond or connection with you. Lastly, they might be genuinely concerned, knowing that this renovation will not only add to your comfort and peace of mind but also to your safety.

■ **Remembering people are layered.** As you pick up on a couple of intuitive threads, remember that people have subconscious and shadow drives and desires that they are not even aware of. They also have old wounds—from past relationships, old traumas, and childhood, most commonly—that create deeply embedded patterns in them that become like a reflex reaction.

■ **Staying humble and acknowledging other people's sovereignty.** Just because you are very intuitive, it does not mean you have all the answers. When friends, or clients, ask you for your intuitive advice, first remind them of this fact. You're only human, and you're fallible. Also empower others to rely on their own intuition, viewing your insights as mere possibilities and food for thought. Tuning in to someone else is a wonderful way to get to the bottom of what might really be going on with them. Remember to simply ask people as well, and don't just assume your intuition is one-hundred-percent accurate or has filled in all the blanks. Also take whatever actions are obvious and practical—just like you would prepare your house for a winter storm even if your intuition told you that this storm may not be that bad. Intuition is meant to help catch your blind sides, not create more of them!

Some things that are *not* useful when trying to tune in to someone else:

■ **Having an agenda or already believing you know best.** If you are sure your preconceived assumptions are right before you tune in with your intuition, are clinging to what you want your intuition to reveal, or are trying to put boundaries and restrictions on your intuition in any way, tuning in will not be that helpful. In fact, you could end up getting a bad or inaccurate intuitive hit, and then only discover the truth when you act on it and learn you were way off base.

- **Being distracted.** Tuning in with your intuition requires focus. Not the kind of focus you use when cramming for an exam, but the kind of focus where you clear your mind of other topics and stay open. Intense emotions can be distracting, as well as having lots of other people or physical stimuli around. That's why one of the best times to tune in to someone is when you're feeling calm and centered, and there's not a lot of physical stimuli or other people's energy in your environment, like when you're taking a quiet walk or calmly cleaning the kitchen when everyone else has gone to bed.

- **Finding it difficult to concentrate.** In our modern world where there are so many distractions and our collective attention span can be the twenty seconds it takes to read an Instagram post, concentration might be something you need to practice. Or you may naturally be wired in a way that keeps concentration from coming as easily for you. For sessions with clients, I meditate on the client for twenty minutes before getting on the phone with them for over an hour. For ninety minutes, not much else enters my mind besides my client and their issues. This is not necessary for you to get intuitive hits on someone, yet practicing being able to quiet your mind so you can focus on another person for ten minutes is ideal. It's easier to concentrate when you enjoy the task at hand, so make using your intuition as enjoyable as possible!

- **Falsely believing you can "predict" the future.** There are many reasons that predicting the future is extremely difficult. People's free-will choices and the chaotic, ever-changing nature of life on Earth can be very challenging to predict. You might sense some possible outcomes for yourself or others in the future, but leave trying to accurately predict the future aside.

If all four of these "don'ts" are stuff you regularly have difficulty with, *don't* worry! Consider these issues a priority to gently work on. Do a puzzle to practice concentration, quiet your mind by having fewer thoughts during routine activities like grocery shopping to limit distraction, mindfully come to situations and relationships with a flexible attitude to practice not pushing an agenda, and remind yourself that unpredictable forces and free-will choices can be a real part of daily life.

TUNE IN TO SOMEONE ELSE WITH YOUR INTUITION

STEP 1: Don't overly complicate this. However, if you have any rituals that traditionally help you tune in, like holding a favorite pocket-size stone or crystal to aid focus, have that handy. Otherwise just quiet your mind and steady your breathing. Make sure you're in a low-stimulation setting—not too much distraction from other people or loud background noise. You can be sitting still (like on your porch or in your study), or you can be moving (like walking or showering).

STEP 2: Think of the person you want to tune in to. Now get curious about what's going on with them—put all your preconceived notions, or even info they have previously shared with you—aside for now. Stay open-minded and neutral.

STEP 3: Recognize any hits coming from your four primary psychic pathways—feeling, hearing, seeing, and knowing guidance. Don't fight or argue with the information coming in. The more you can let it flow and not resist, the more productive this tune-in session will be.

STEP 4: When you're ready, gently switch focus to something else by taking your mind to another subject, maybe something mundane like chores or work deadlines. Pay attention to the physical stimuli around you—the smell of fresh-cut grass, the feel of soap lather on your skin, the sounds coming from the next room—to bring yourself more into the present moment. Keep in mind that intuitive insights about someone else can come to you organically anytime. The important ones will surface whether you're mindfully focusing and tuning in or not.

STEP 5: Later on, review the intuitive hits you received. Those that came in initially, as well as those that keep coming back to mind throughout the day randomly, can be most important. How many threads did you pick up on? How many layers of this person's psyche might you have gained brief access to?

STEP 6: Before acting on your intuitive guidance, gather more data and empirical evidence from sources outside your intuition. This is important! Remember that your intuition is fallible. Be open to other intuitive interpretations too over time (as situations and people are always shifting and transforming organically), and take a balanced, measured, cautious approach. This is not the same as discounting your intuition, just being a responsible custodian of it.

> ### MANTRA
> Tuning in to someone else can be a fun, informative way to practice using my intuition more intentionally. There are always many layers and threads, as well as different possibilities in the future, so I remain open, curious, and flexible.

WHAT'S YOUR RELATIONSHIP WITH YOUR OWN INTUITION?

Answer the following questions with: very true, sometimes true, or rarely true. *Do not* read the answer key first! It's a natural impulse that I'm guilty of too. But acting on that impulse really might ruin this quiz for you.

Try to answer honestly, with self-compassion and without judgment. That will help you make the most of the answer key. There really are no right or wrong answers here, which will become obvious by the end.

1. My intuitive hunches are something I mindfully incorporate into my decision-making process.

2. When someone makes fun of the sixth sense, or minimizes its power, I may not say anything out loud, but inwardly I roll my eyes and think, "Wow, they are really misinformed."

3. I practice using my intuition more intentionally with exercises or rituals or by playing fun, harmless games to test my intuition.

4. My intuition is only one of the ways I navigate the world, and I equally value my emotions, logic, the opinion of experts, and the wisdom of my own past experiences.

5. In general, I'm familiar with the four clairs or primary psychic pathways. If they are not all open and active in me, I know which ones I'm strongest in right now.

6. I've had a previously dormant psychic pathway open or become much stronger. I'm enjoying this increased level of intuitive ability!

7. Intuitive mentors are people I follow on social media, take workshops from, or read articles and books by so I can keep learning about and growing my intuition.

8. There's always more to understand about the sixth sense, and I believe no single person or source has access to all the answers or knowledge about it.

9. I honestly feel my intuition has the capacity to improve and grow. That's not as scary to me as it is exciting.

10. Just because the way I receive intuitive hits isn't exactly like the way other people do, I remind myself that my intuition is powerful and valuable. I believe that I'm intuitively wired the way I am for a reason, and I trust this.

11. I'd say that part of loving and valuing myself is valuing my intuition. Rejecting my sixth sense feels like rejecting part of me.

12. I can sense when to share my intuitive hits among family, friends, and colleagues who are open to intuition, and I can sense when to keep things to myself.

13. Consulting my intuition is an organic reflex that I don't have to think about ahead of time, like muscle memory when I'm riding a bike.

14. Taking good care of myself physically is a priority for me.

15. I go through busy times, but in general I try to schedule downtime and live my life at a gentle, even pace.

16. I try not to deny or stuff down my emotions, and I have methods to process my emotions and uncover the jewels of wisdom buried within them.

17. There are times each day when I try to prioritize light, playful energy!

18. I regularly practice quieting my mind or trying to have fewer thoughts.

19. Even when it's uncomfortable, I'm pretty good about standing my ground and saying "no" to others or following my own inner wisdom when that seems best.

20. Divination tools like runes, astrology, numerology, the I Ching, and oracle or tarot cards intrigue me, and I have at least one that I like to consult on occasion.

21. I have a relationship to Spirit in a form that resonates with me, whether that's feeling connected to an angel, spirit guide, departed loved one, my own soul, a higher power, or something else, and I feel that this benevolent force sometimes sends me intuitive guidance.

22. I regularly receive meaningful signs or synchronicities as intuitive guidance. These come to me in all manner of ways, so I don't limit my intuition by expecting those signs to always show up in the exact same way.

23. Sometimes I'll have a dream as intuitive guidance, where I get helpful information I could not have known any other way or someone from the other side connects with me.

24. I realize my intuition isn't perfect, and when I get something wrong I'm generally able to shrug it off and try again.

25. I'm open and flexible about how I approach my life, and that helps me be more open about options presented to me by my intuition.

26. I've had intuition or sensitivity growth spurts in the past, and this feels normal to me or is something I now have tools to manage.

ANSWERED MOSTLY "VERY TRUE":

The pros: You really value your intuition and have a strong sixth sense, as well as possessing a commanding knowledge of how intuition works. That's cause for celebration and congratulations! You're an excellent ambassador or PR person for intuition, so please encourage others to trust and keep developing their sixth sense—*if* they're open to hearing this! You're likely very comfortable with your intuition growing and deepening, an open attitude that will facilitate an even more dynamic, robust intuition as time goes on.

The cons: Remember that everyone's intuition has a blind spot—just like the blind spots that appear when driving a car. The real danger when you have a naturally strong intuition, a good handle on its working mechanics, and a deep trust in your sixth sense, is that you can become overconfident or even arrogant (this is something I have to watch out for). Healthy skepticism about your own intuitive hits is also valuable. You too can fall prey to your own desires, intense emotions, or preconceived notions overriding or tricking your intuition. And there are simply some things that are very hard, or impossible, to predict. Remember that people, their free-will choices, and outside forces are constantly evolving organically. Often the most you can predict are possibilities. Sharpening, understanding, and mastering intuition is a lifetime's work that's never perfect!

Recommended action: Get in the habit of asking others for their intuitive take on your life. Even with clients who are very intuitive, I'll always pick up on intuitive threads in a session that they have not yet considered. This does not mean you have to come to me, or pay anyone, for an intuitive second opinion. You can identify intuitive family members, friends, and colleagues who can provide intuitive insight, and then do the same for them in return! Even after getting the intuitive opinion of others and processing that, it's best to make your own decisions and go with what feels right to you when the dust settles. Remember that logic and empirical evidence should be considered as well.

ANSWERED MOSTLY "SOMETIMES TRUE":

The pros: You understand the value of healthy skepticism, even about your own intuitive hits. Perhaps you're the kind of person who always takes things with a grain of salt, consults several sources when seeking answers, enjoys researching, and looks at an issue from all angles. That's a very practical, admirable, balanced approach! You also know intuition is real, and that you have it. This puts you far ahead of many people regarding making the most of the sixth sense.

The cons: While it's great that you approach your intuitive hits in an even-keeled, measured fashion, you may not be placing enough value on them and therefore not getting the full benefit of your sixth sense. This in itself can stunt intuitive growth as well. Your sixth sense can only flourish if you give it a little more lead or rope. Remember, you don't have to be perfect with your intuitive hits, or be a professional intuitive, or have exceptional intuitive ability to place high value on your own sixth sense. Your intuition requires validation from you, and an acknowledgment that it's intimately connected to you and your concerns, and deserves respect and attention more than—or at least as much as—any force outside yourself.

Recommended action: Practice taking actions that are based on your intuitive hits. Making decisions based on your intuition when you don't have as much skin in the game—like where to go for lunch, or what route to take on your commute home, or whom to pick up the phone and reach out to—can be a great way to practice. Remember to maintain a playful energy and have fun with the process, as placing too much stress or judgment on your intuition will impede its powers and inhibit optimal performance. Sometimes when you possess a good basic knowledge of a subject, the only way to learn more, gain confidence, and achieve mastery is to step outside your comfort zone and put your knowledge into practice.

ANSWERED MOSTLY "RARELY TRUE":

The pros: Thank you for being so honest in your answers—applaud yourself for this! It takes courage to admit you're not as comfortable or confident about something. The good news about landing in this category is you may have no clue how powerful or varied your own intuition might be. Natural intuitive ability exists on a spectrum, and since you're likely not yet aware enough to be engaging yours actively, you may very well be at the higher end of that intuitive spectrum! No matter where you are on the intuition spectrum now, you can improve dramatically in time with awareness and practice. Beginning the journey of discovering your intuitive ability can be a really magical time full of wonder and delight, so in some ways I'm envious of you for being at this stage!

The cons: Your sixth sense is an important part of your natural navigational or GPS system. Without trusting and understanding it, you're missing out on great insights that could make you a more powerful co-creator as well as make your Earthly life, at times, a smoother journey. By not utilizing and maximizing your sixth sense, you're leaving a lot on the table. You might put too much value on the intuitive insights of others, and not anchor into your own intuition for guidance enough. Being centered in yourself and your sixth sense is always where you are most powerful!

Recommended action: The best way to demystify something is to learn more about it. If you're new to anything—a healing modality, a culture or language, or intuition—it can be intimidating and even a little scary. Learn all you can about intuition to empower yourself and feel more comfortable with the sixth sense. Once you understand more, that will build your confidence to begin using your intuition more proactively. While you research all the amazing potential of intuition, make sure to also become familiar with the guardrails. This will make you feel safer and more grounded about beginning to recognize and heed your intuitive hunches! Go back and re-read the section in this book on gut instincts. Practice discerning yours more.

Advice for all categories: There's always room for improvement regarding your intuition. Use your intuition now to identify what you personally could benefit from working on. Ask your sixth sense to pick three numbers from 1 to 26, one at a time, and then read the corresponding statements in the quiz. These particular statements contain some element of growth potential for you regarding your intuition. You could receive the numbers as a voice in your mind, a picture in your mind, or you can scan the numbers and notice when you feel a strong energetic pull to a certain number. My intuition directed me to the number 4, about remembering that my intuition, while important, is only one of the ways I navigate the world. I'm betting I need to place more value on my emotions. They provide essential clues about what to focus on regarding my destiny; what's frustrating me and needs to be reviewed and revised in my life; when I need to set better boundaries or stand my ground; and what brings me joy or contentment and should be prioritized. Which numbers/statements did your intuition guide you to?

Chapter 4

♥

Nurturing Your Relationships

There's a lot of emphasis in the empath community on setting boundaries, prioritizing yourself, and creating healthy space from others and the world—all important stuff we've been covering in this book! There is good reason for this emphasis: empaths' unique sensitivity allows them to intimately feel others' energy and emotions in their own system, which means that empaths require special relationship tools to help them *separate* in a healthy way. That was the inspiration for this book, and probably part of why you were drawn to it.

Yet as much as empaths need to learn how and when to mindfully separate, they also long to connect! When you can feel other people's energies and emotions—as well as the energies and emotions of the collective—in your own system, you are capable of bonding with people in general intimately and deeply . . . and perhaps even naturally wired to do so for a reason. We can all agree that there are downsides or challenges to being an empath—just like there are challenges to anything. Since you surely have dealt with those drawbacks as part of your experience with sensitivity, you might as well get the full benefit of the extraordinary blessings of being an empath!

This chapter is designed to help you do just that, to strengthen your bonds with others so you can soak up all the yummy stuff in your relationships—like taking a piece of bread, dragging it across your plate, and soaking up all the savory sauce. The following sections and exercises aim to identify ways in which sensitive people may particularly enjoy bonding with others, as well as to provide more broad advice on creating and nurturing intimacy.

Establishing Nourishing Relationship Routines

We've already established the value of healthy routines for empaths many times in this book. Routine can be incredibly stabilizing to your sensitive system, and it can also stabilize your relationships. As an empath who is naturally good at picking up on what others want and need, part of nurturing your relationships is making sure your needs are met too. So if you're a sensitive person who loves the grounded energy of regular routine, make sure to establish nourishing routines with the people you value most in your life.

Nourishing relationship routines might. . . .

- **Happen regularly or establish a predictable rhythm**, like a daily text with a partner, a weekly gym workout with a family member, a biweekly coffee date with a close friend, or a monthly lunch or video conference with a group of colleagues.
- **Be flexible**, so that if someone is overwhelmed and needs more space, or is struggling and needs more support, the routine can be adjusted. There can be an organic fluctuation to your routines. If a sibling usually calls you during their evening walk after work, it could be nice to establish that you only pick up when you have time and energy, and they only call when they have time and energy.

- **Maintain a theme but avoid boredom**, like going for brunch with your partner on the weekends, but regularly trying out new places in new neighborhoods.
- **Need to work well for all involved**, like discovering that your book club likes to meet at the same spot for dinner once a month because its location is very convenient for everyone, the price is affordable, and the staff enjoys seeing you there.
- **Be engaging enough to deepen the bond**, like meeting up with another film buff to attend a screening once a month, but then hanging out afterward for coffee or wine to discuss the themes and what you did and didn't enjoy about the film.
- **Help the other person feel seen or valued**, which could require you to step outside your comfort zone. If you and a girlfriend usually go dancing at a certain type of club to a certain type of music, but she wants to try country line dancing, it could be deeply nourishing for the friendship if you accompany her.
- **Be allowed to end or evolve**, which is very natural. If an old friend moves across the country to a town where they know no one, a longer weekly video chat on the weekends might be something they really look forward to initially. In time, as they lay down roots and meet people locally, the routine might naturally fall away or transform.

Whether it's with family, friends, colleagues, or people who share your passion for a hobby or cause or lifestyle, establishing routines with others is an ideal way to nourish your relationships and your sensitive system at the same time!

IMPLEMENT ONE NEW RELATIONSHIP ROUTINE

STEP 1: Identify relationships that you would like to strengthen or deepen, as well as activities you enjoy. This could be with one other person (like a child or roommate), or a group of people (like colleagues working in the same field or a larger family group).

STEP 2: Consider what you *all* enjoy doing or your common ground. You and your children might all love to play basketball, you and a group of friends might all enjoy attending spiritual workshops, you and your partner might like to listen to funny memoirs read aloud or funny podcasts, you and your parent might both love to sit at coffee shops and do the crossword, or you and a group of neighbors might all pick up trash on the beach.

STEP 3: See if you can start a club among a group of people—like a monthly professional networking breakfast or monthly singles hike or weekly volunteer commitment—and let folks know they can show up week to week or month to month as much or as little as they like (some will come every time, and some will pop in and out). Or see if you can set a time for individuals or a smaller group of people to meet regularly— like a weekly family dinner at a local diner, or a monthly afternoon lunch and yoga date with a friend. Let people know you'd love to make this a regular hang session, but that it's flexible based on people's availability and schedule each day, week, or month.

> ## MANTRA:
> Regular routines with important people both cement bonds and stabilize my sensitive system. The key is being flexible with schedules and trying to make routine activities nourishing for everyone.

Acknowledging and Validating Other People's Emotions

Feeling with other people can be a lot—especially if what the other person is feeling is intense or very challenging. Yet showing up for others and standing by them during the difficult or intense seasons of their lives is a foundational component of strong relationships. Many times, folks just want to know that they are not alone with their intense emotions or life circumstances. And part of what makes the good times good is being able to share your emotional experience with others. Yet if empaths open up to feel everything with others when emotions are running high, it could easily overwhelm and exhaust a sensitive system. When sensitive empaths have proper tools, it can be easier to remain present and show up for loved ones consistently.

Acknowledging someone else's emotions is an amazing gift to offer anyone in your life, whether they are experiencing an intense emotional high—like getting their dream job the same month they buy their dream home—or they're experiencing an emotional low—like having a close family member pass the same month they learn that they didn't get into any of the colleges they applied to. *Validating* another person's emotions—or not requiring them to qualify or justify an emotion—while offering moments of real presence, might be the best support. After all, there is a deep, natural need in humans to simply feel seen.

As a sensitive person, it can be seductive to believe you should fix or change someone's problems or issues, or tamp down their emotions. Your subconscious might decide that this is the best way to put out the emotional fire to protect both them and you—since you can feel with the other person. Remember that feelings don't need to be fixed—just acknowledged and validated. That combo is a powerful cooling agent! Other people may not need you to have all the answers about how to live their lives. They may just need you to love and stand by them while they figure it out for themselves.

Acknowledging and validating looks like:

- **Stating to the other person what it seems like they are feeling.** If you're not sure if they are more sad or more angry, for example, just say something like, "You're upset. This has been a lot, and you must be feeling so many emotions right now."

- **Being sure to have language in your statement that reflects this is *their* feeling and their situation, not yours.** "I'm here for you during your job loss. I know it must be tough for you." This will remind you not to take on the emotion or issue as if it were your own.

- **Letting the other person tell you what they need, instead of taking ownership of their life and assuming.** You might ask, "How can I support you now?" This helps to keep them in the driver's seat and you in the passenger seat, or witnessing/observer mode and centered in your own energy.

- **Reminding the other person that you don't know exactly how they feel, and you're not pretending to.** "I can't imagine what this is like for you!" is something you might say if the other person is having a big win and they are idling high. This also invites the other person to do some emotional processing by sharing what they are feeling.

- **Doing more listening than talking.** When you talk, keep it simple and straightforward. What you are mainly offering is grounded presence. That can be incredibly supportive when people are going through intense times.

- **Reminding the other person that their feelings make sense and are understandable—in other words, their feelings are valid.** This is the opposite of having to justify a feeling. If the other person wants to explain their feelings or give context, that's great. But don't require it.

> ▪ Keeping a foot in your discerning claircognizant psychic pathway, where you are allowed to be detached in a healthy way. You can also have moments where feeling with them is helpful or nourishing to both of you, or you can keep verbalizing your connection in a grounded way.

I've learned so much about the simple, yet astoundingly effective, art of acknowledging and validating emotions from my friend and colleague Natasha Levinger, author of *Healing Your Inner Child*. Try this not only with others, but with yourself when you are feeling and processing something intense.

PRACTICE ACKNOWLEDGING & VALIDATING EMOTIONS WITH YOURSELF

STEP 1: The next time you're feeling an intense emotion, stop and *acknowledge* the emotion by identifying and naming it, like joy, anxiety, elation, disappointment.

STEP 2: Instead of going into your head to make sense of the emotion, justify it, or explain to yourself why you are feeling this, simply put your hand over your physical heart. Take a few breaths and connect to your energetic heart. Then *validate* the emotion by reminding yourself, silently, "I'm afraid" or "I'm thrilled!" Remind yourself this is real, and it is what it is. Don't argue with the emotion or critique it. Giving context to your emotion and analyzing it can happen organically later.

STEP 3: Notice if simply acknowledging and validating the emotion makes it easier to sit with, or makes you feel comforted. We can spend a lot of time and energy running from our emotions, which could make them stronger to get our attention, or cause us to act them out in confusing ways.

STEP 4: Once you feel seen emotionally by yourself, ask yourself, "How can I best support *me* right now?" Let your intuition and higher self supply the answers! If you're experiencing a trauma or experiencing PTSD from a past trauma, make sure that one of the ways you support yourself is by reaching out to others for help. Always reach out for help if an emotion is scaring you or you feel out of control. Supporting yourself while you're feeling something intense is an amazing way to nurture yourself. Doing something simple in the moment to comfort yourself—like snuggling up with your favorite pillows and your favorite music—can be very helpful whether what you're feeling is challenging or joyful.

> **MANTRA**
> I can practice acknowledging and validating the feelings of others by doing this for myself. The final step is always asking myself what support I require.

Collecting Objects of Affection

Empaths are not only sensitive to the energy of spaces, they are sensitive to the energy of objects. While objects might carry or store energy, objects also create associations with people, places, and memories. This is why objects can be so precious to us, whether it's a stone you've charged with healing energy that helped ground you during a difficult year, a favorite blanket your late grandmother made that you snuggle to feel closer to her, or the "lucky" power jacket you wear to important meetings. Objects can contain energy, but certain objects can also create certain energies inside us.

Many empaths can be very sensitive to their surroundings, so being surrounded by objects that fit your aesthetic could create a lovely vibe in your home. This is a vibe that people may pick up on when they visit you—even if they don't share your same taste or decorating style! Whether you like a clean minimalist look or are a knickknack fanatic (that's me!), or whether you live in a huge, rambling farmhouse or a tiny, cute apartment in the city, you can create an energy in your living space that makes you feel more connected to people you care about.

Objects of affection might. . . .

- **Be something you collected on a trip with a loved one**, like seashells gathered with a child while walking the beach or a pretty vase bought while on a weekend getaway with a good friend.
- **Remind you of a loved one who has passed**, like a favorite picture in a special frame or a ring that you wear that belonged to them.
- **Change or grow**, like a clipping from a loved one's garden that you plant in a windowsill pot, or a large candle that someone gives you for New Year's that lasts for months.
- **Be very ordinary**, like a set of bowls you and a roommate found on sale after you'd just rented your first place.
- **Be wonderfully imperfect**, like the "ugly" sweater you wore on a magical camping trip with a group of college friends and now can't bear to part with.
- **Remind you of an important time or mile marker**, like a wedding photo or a photo of you and a friend at your high school graduation.
- **Create a tradition**, like buying a new piece of pottery every year for an anniversary or getting a sibling a new T-shirt that immortalizes one of their favorite musicians each year for their birthday.
- **Capture a memory**, like framing tickets that you and your child used to attend a big sports game together or wearing the baseball cap with the name of the beach you had a great family vacation at.

■ **Utilize creativity and be handmade**, like a piece of art you make for someone's garden or the bookmark a child bedazzles for you at their summer-camp crafting class.

Anytime you give someone a gift, remember this is a chance to give them an object of affection that could strengthen your bond, like a coffee mug they might reach for when they're missing you or feeling down and need a lift. Take into account the other person's style, and it can be nice to choose an object that somehow connects you or represents your relationship or a shared memory or interest. If you're missing someone, or you're upset with someone and wanting to soften your energy toward them, displaying an object of affection that reminds you of them can be very healing!

IDENTIFY OBJECTS OF AFFECTION

STEP 1: Look around your space, and identify some objects of affection that make you feel connected to people you care about. This could be clothing, furniture, blankets and rugs, plants (which are alive), knickknacks, art, photos, dishes, pottery, pillows, jewelry, books, or anything else.

STEP 2: The next time you're missing someone, feeling challenging emotions about a loved one, or feeling lonely in general, get out an object of affection that makes you feel connected to that person or brings back a lovely memory of connection with someone special, and place it prominently in your space. That could be on your desk, in the middle of your kitchen table, stuck to the bathroom mirror or the fridge, or beside your bed so you see it before you fall asleep.

STEP 3: The next time you have the excuse to get someone a gift, make it count. Remember, objects of affection don't have to cost much, or any, money. Finding a biography of a friend's favorite historical figure or a 45 rpm record of their favorite artist in the bargain bin could become a treasured object of affection.

> **MANTRA**
> Money can't buy love, but certain objects can inspire affection and increase connection between myself and the people I care about.

Learning the Empath Love Language

You may have heard the theory that there are five love languages, or ways people like to express and receive affection—through healthy physical touch, through words of affirmation, through acts of service, through gifts, and through spending quality time together. For a combination of reasons—like the environment you were raised in, your past traumas, and your innate personality—you might prefer one or two over the others. The same is true for the people in your life, so sometimes learning another's predominant love language or languages can truly have a profound positive impact on the quality of your relationship with them.

I wanted to also introduce a sixth love language in this book, *grace*, one that empaths in particular could benefit from learning and utilizing, since grace is interpreted through the sixth sense.

- Grace is a spiritual or unseen force that seems to step in and aid humans.
- Grace is a benevolent force that does not have to be earned or asked for.
- Grace often shows up on its own, yet it can also be called in.

- Grace checks your blind spot, helps you when you are in a tight spot, and brings things into your life when the timing is ideal.
- Grace works best when you can be open and surrender, as grace might know what you need in the moment more than you do.

For sensitive empaths who are naturally intuitive, grace is the perfect relationship ally as it makes itself known to us via the sixth sense. Grace could be a synchronicity that softens you, like turning on the radio and hearing the opening notes of your wedding song when you're furious with your partner. Or grace could be an intuitive nudge, whispering that you should tell a colleague about the project you're launching because she's actually looking to invest time and money into just such a project.

Based on my personal experience and my experience working with clients regarding their relationships, it's valuable to learn someone else's love language(s), partly because we often have different love languages than the people we love. I enjoy giving and receiving via all the love languages, yet I think my primary language is acts of service—I show people I love them by cleaning the kitchen every night! I also enjoy giving gifts, a love language I believe I learned from my grandmother Marguerite. My partner prefers touch (like a good foot massage) and words of affirmation (he's always telling me how much he loves me).

Because of these differences, other people can actually help you appreciate other love languages. You might have a friend who really values spending quality time together, so making space in your schedule for regular hang sessions is important to that relationship. Or you might have a parent who really values giving and receiving gifts, so with this person it's important to mark special occasions by offering them an object of affection. In turn, they can learn to recognize and appreciate your love language(s).

Of course, people are very complex, and relationships are also complex. When you're not sure about someone's preferred love language(s), you're not sure what this particular relationship or moment calls for, or you want to practice using your intuition, employ the sixth love language of grace.

Use the empath love language of grace by:

- **Surrendering**, staying open, and silently asking the benevolent force of grace how best to show your affection for this person right now.
- **Waiting for a synchronicity**—like getting an email alert that concert tickets for their favorite band have just gone on sale. Going to the concert with them would represent the love language of spending quality time together.
- **Waiting for an intuitive nudge**—like feeling a pull toward the flower section of the grocery store as you're grabbing a few items for your partner on your way home from work. Getting your partner some flowers would represent the love language of gifts.

PRACTICE GIVING GRACE

STEP 1: The next time you want to show someone affection, get curious and ask grace to give you guidance through your sixth sense.

STEP 2: Stay open and surrender as you wait for intuitive guidance to arrive. It could come immediately, or it could take a few hours or days.

STEP 3: Act on this guidance. You might hear "words of affirmation" in your mind when wondering how to express love to a sibling. Grace's suggestion? Tell them by offering a thoughtful compliment in person or sending them a hand-written card in the mail. You might get a synchronicity in the form of a coupon for a massage so you can offer your spouse the gift of healthy touch. Or you might feel an intuitive nudge to take an afternoon off work for a hang session with a child so you can spend quality time together. Whatever the intuitive guidance from grace is, be sure to take an action step! The flow of grace is increased by following its guidance.

> **MANTRA**
> There are so many ways to show affection to people I care about. As a sensitive person, I can use my own intuition to discern how.

Giving What You Want to Receive

Sometimes a relationship needs to end, and other times it's simply the dynamic of how people show up in the relationship that needs to end. As an empath who is sensitive to energy, being more conscious of the energy you bring to a relationship can help upgrade a relationship dynamic. People often mirror the energy they are met with, so the empath Jedi mind trick of giving people what you want to receive can be a transformational tool worth trying on struggling relationships.

If you're wanting a business colleague to show you more respect and gratitude, make sure to treat them respectfully when they share their ideas and tell them regularly how much you value them and your collaboration. If you're wanting more warmth and tenderness in your life in general, treat the people you interact with warmly and tenderly, whether that's being kind to a customer-service person you call for assistance or being sweet to a family member you call to say hello.

Giving what you want to receive is different than overgiving. It's more about quality than quantity. Giving what you want to receive is an energy dance where you are inviting someone into a different energy dynamic. They may accept the invitation—or not. Remember, it can take time for the other person to pick up on the rhythm of this new energy, or they might recognize it, welcome it, and begin grooving with you immediately. People who are more sensitive to energy will often pick up the new steps to this different energy dance quickly.

This technique can upgrade the energy in a current relationship, as well as attract a different type of energy and relationship to you.

Or giving what you want to receive can get you crystal-clear on what another person is prepared to give or even capable of giving. Remember, this is not about being a martyr or putting up with bad behavior from others: it's about seeing if you can shift the energy of a relationship like a Jedi master to something more fulfilling, nourishing, and healthy for both people.

UPGRADE THE ENERGY DYNAMIC IN A RELATIONSHIP

STEP 1: Decide what you want to receive in a relationship, and name it. Examples include: attention, patience, understanding, compassion, forgiveness, recognition.

STEP 2: Begin giving that to the other person, group of people, or people in general. Notice how you have to show up with a different energy to do that, and notice how, to create this energy, your behavior, motivation, tone of voice, or body language changes as well.

STEP 3: Observe if this has any immediate or noticeable effect on others. It may not, which is valuable information and makes the exercise worth your time. Yet it can take time for this new energy dynamic you are creating to take full effect. Be patient, as others and the world around you gradually recalibrate because of your new energy.

MANTRA
When I want to be treated a certain way, I identify how I can treat others and the world that way myself to court this energy and draw it into my life.

Opening Up to Feel with Others

Being an empath is a balancing act of opening up to feel with and enjoy your sensitivity, and of pulling back to protect your sensitivity. There are times when a loved one is feeling all the feels, whether that's healing joy and celebration or devastating sorrow and anger. You always have the option of pulling back to protect yourself and supporting them from a place of healthy, compassionate, grounded detachment—truly a gift to offer anyone in your life. I've presented tools in this book to empower you to pull back and protect your sensitivity. Yet there are times when the most nourishing option might be to open up with your clairsentient psychic pathway and feel with others.

Once a dear friend's family member suffered a life-changing injury. I was with my friend when she received the phone call and found out the news. She was heartbroken, terrified, and briefly inconsolable. There was a question in her eyes and a confused expression on her face that said, "How do I hold all this?" Something in me whispered that opening up to feel with her, and holding some of that pain too, would bolster her spirit for what was to come. I was so glad I could support her that day, and that I was feeling physically strong and emotionally stable enough to open up to all that challenging emotion and help carry a little, for a short time, to lighten her load.

Many years later, another friend did the same for me when I bought my first home, which was not only a joyful event but also a very healing one. As a child and teen, I had been bounced around and kicked out of many homes; and while I rented a fabulous yet tiny apartment in Manhattan for decades with my husband as an adult, I'd always dreamed of owning a traditional home. When I moved out of the city, I was able to pull off this mini-miracle; and the first time I had a video chat with this old friend in my new home office, she started to compliment me on how pretty the space looked, and then started crying. "You have wanted this for so long," she said through sobs. Her tears warmed my heart. I felt so seen, as if I hadn't gone through all those years of struggle alone. As an old friend, she knew my history with homes, and now she knew the complex emotions I was feeling. My childhood suffering and years of longing were very much on my mind, yet they made my joy now more profound, and her tears let me know she really understood.

In sessions with clients, I will receive clairsentient physical cues, like getting chills all over my body if my intuition is informing me that something myself or the client has said is very important to consider. Although I maintain a witnessing/observer mode of healthy detachment, as that's the best way to pull in as much guidance as I can for my client in our short time together, there are instances when I may feel with them—tears coming to my eyes and my voice cracking with emotion. This usually only happens if we begin discussing a loved one who has passed.

As soon as I feel my clairsentience automatically kick in this way, it's just a few seconds before I gather myself and ground back into healthy detachment. While feeling into possibilities in a client's life with my clairsentience is helpful (a possibility in their career might feel light or heavy, or a romantic possibility might feel exciting or dull), I don't try to feel my client's emotions with them. Healthy emotional detachment is always the best way for me to support a client, and it might be the best way for you to support a loved one. When your energetic heart instinctively opens up to feel, you have the choice to pivot if you are too overwhelmed to feel with others or if you sense that feeling with them is not the most supportive choice. Yet, at times, mindfully opening up to feel with others can be a deeply connecting, supportive act that nurtures your relationships.

MINDFULLY FEEL WITH ANOTHER

STEP 1: Whether it happens organically in the moment, or an ideal moment presents itself to try this exercise, practice intentionally feeling with someone else. They might be celebrating something fun and exciting, or navigating a heartbreak, but don't fight it when you begin to feel some of their emotions in your own system.

STEP 2: Keep one foot on the ground as you step into their emotional experience by reminding yourself that this is not your life or your circumstances. Even when feeling someone else's emotions in your own system, the other person is still in actuality separate from you. The golden rule remains: *if it's too overwhelming, pull back into healthy detachment and neutral energy.*

STEP 3: Once you have supported someone by feeling with them, and your interaction is over, take your thoughts and focus elsewhere—make this a regular practice that begins to feel instinctive. If you're walking away from a lunch date with them, notice what's happening on the street as you approach the subway, your car, or your bike. Take your thoughts elsewhere by deliberately focusing on something in *your* life that's neutral—like pondering what errands you need to run this weekend or what new show or novel series you want to start next.

When you feel with someone, and then can pivot quickly back to your life and a neutral subject, you can actually feel much lighter and calmer after your encounter. This is similar to how you can feel much lighter and calmer after having a cleansing cry when you're upset or having a good belly laugh when you are happy. The sense of emotional release—whether you are feeling your feelings or opening up to feel with someone else—can be the same.

> ## MANTRA
> Feeling with others can be healing for everyone involved. Yet I always have to maintain vigilant healthy boundaries around this empath ability, like putting time limits on how long I stay so intimately connected.

Sending Someone Loving Energy

As an empath who is sensitive to energy, you have probably already experienced energy's mysterious, undeniable effect. Besides being able to sense the energy of a room, the collective energy of a group, or the energy of an individual, some empaths may be good at creating energy and even sending it to others.

Not long ago, I was at a family reunion, and the property we were staying on was also home to a group of small donkeys. When one of my relatives was getting ready to leave at the end of the trip, the curious donkeys surrounded his car. "I really have to get going," he muttered. "I told my office I'd be able to show up for a half day this afternoon."

Trying to be helpful, I channeled my inner cowboy, took off my hat, and began waving the donkeys away from his car. "Come on, now, sweethearts, move along," I said, standing several feet away from the car and attempting to herd them toward me. They did not move an inch. This went on for ten frustrating minutes. These donkeys were so mellow and adorable, yet incredibly stubborn—or so it seemed.

I wonder what would happen if I changed my energy, I thought. Switching tactics, I put my hat back on and remained still, feeling my energy body come alive. This could feel like gentle pressure, slight warmth, mild tingling, or any other subtle change in your physical body. I made my energy very soft. Without saying a word, or making any physical movement, I directed loving energy toward the donkeys. What happened next was remarkable, and even surprised me. Within thirty seconds, all the donkeys turned and slowly walked over to me. They began sniffing me and snuggling in very close to me.

My relative was amazed. "Wow!" he said. "Tanya, the donkey whisperer!" The path was now clear for him to safely back out his car . . . and I had made a herd of new friends.

Sending someone else loving energy might be something the other person, who is receiving, isn't consciously aware of but may still sense or experience in a positive way. Sending someone else loving energy might soften their own energy, soften them toward you, or make them feel more comforted, supported, or hopeful. Some reasons you might send someone else loving energy include:

- **Because someone you know is upset or anxious**, and, after listening, acknowledging and validating their emotions, offering advice, and doing any other practical, helpful action, you're not sure what else to do to support them.

- **To make yourself feel better** because you are worried about someone else.

- **Because you no longer have contact with this person**, and it would be inappropriate to reach out in another way, but you want to wish them well.

- **To honor the idea that we each have a soul**, or a spiritual side to ourselves—if that concept resonates with you. In this case, sending loving energy would be a type of prayer from your soul to theirs.

- **Because you cannot talk to someone, as they are unavailable by modern communication means** (they are taking a big exam, they are in the military and on assignment, they are having an operation), and you want to express your love and support for them.

- **To show symbolically that you forgive them and to release your connection**—especially if you do not want contact with this person or do not want them back in your life.

- **Because the person has passed away** and you want to honor your continued feeling of connection to their spirit.

- **To gain a sense of closure** when a relationship ends.

- **Because you interacted with a stranger** on the street or in a store, or saw someone in the news, who seems like they could use love.

- **Because an acquaintance keeps coming into your mind** and you're not sure why, but you may not know them well enough to reach out.

Sending someone else loving energy is a lovely way to use your unique sensitivity and dole out some good vibes into the world! The collective energy field can always benefit from more of this!

SEND OUT HEALING ENERGY

STEP 1: Love is a healer. And you can simply send loving energy anytime, anywhere. First, focus on the other person, perhaps by thinking of their name or picturing their face in your mind.

STEP 2: Place your hand over your physical heart to connect with your energetic heart. Focus on a loving energy—concentrate on how love feels emotionally. Notice if you see any clairvoyant images in your mind, like a pretty color, a heart-shaped image, or other images. Also notice if you feel any physical sensations like pressure, warmth, or tingles in any part of your body—this may happen as the loving energy you are creating builds. Don't force anything. It's much easier to create this type of energy when you are relaxed.

STEP 3: Now imagine this loving energy washing over the person you are sending it to. Imagine them smiling, or imagine their body relaxing. Picture them in a blissed-out state—like just after a massage or the final meditation of a gentle yoga class. You might see clairvoyant images. If you imagined the loving energy as a color, you might see that color washing over them. Or you might see images of you two from the past, or a healing image from their soul that is outside the bounds of time and space.

STEP 4: As the energy naturally begins to dissipate, take your focus elsewhere. It may only take seconds or a minute or two to do this exercise. Notice if you feel different afterward, like calmer, more peaceful, or more blissful. The loving, healing energy you created is still circulating around and within you!

> **MANTRA**
> I can send loving, healing energy to anyone—including myself!

Being a Friend, Not a Therapist

Are you an empath people automatically open up to? Some sensitive people who are also very tender-hearted *may* find that others start telling them lots of really personal, deep stuff fairly quickly or easily. Many sensitive clients tell me this has happened to them, and it's always been the case for me personally, or since I was a teen.

As an adult who now speaks to clients for intuitive sessions professionally (you may also be a counselor, intuitive, or coach), I probably more than ever give off the energy of someone to confide in. It's very common for people I've just met at a social gathering to talk to me at length, ask for advice, and open up in astonishing ways when they don't even know what I do for a living. I guess they are sensing my energy!

Whether this happens to you with strangers or not, you surely have people in your life who rely on you for support, and sometimes want to talk about themselves a lot! It's natural and healthy for friends, coworkers, and family members to process their emotions and brainstorm options by talking it all through. I know you benefit from being able to do this as well. It's very human and something we all need.

A counselor who offers talk therapy is different than a supportive and kind-hearted friend. Therapists provide a place of sacred presence, facilitate healing, help people discover their patterns, offer clients emotional and mental-health tools, give perspective, and listen with compassion— among other things. Therapists are paid for their time, put limits on how long a session lasts and how frequently sessions happen, and also have other ground rules as well as qualifications. If a friend, family member, or colleague begins confusing you with a professional counselor, it's likely that that person will leave you drained, as well as expect from you what you cannot provide.

If you feel exhausted after talking to someone, find yourself wanting to avoid their calls or texts, or notice that they talk only about themselves and rarely ask about you, try some of the following:

- **Put limits on your availability.** Don't jump to immediately answer their texts, and practice letting their calls go to voicemail.
- **Set time limits on how long you listen.** Glance at the clock when you're on the phone with someone, listen for as long as it takes to unload the dishwasher, or tell them once you sit down to lunch that you can only stay for an hour.
- **Diplomatically and compassionately suggest that they get support from other places**—this individual just may require more right now. That could include any health-care provider, a support group, a life coach, a book by an expert, or different loved ones. Frame your suggestion as coming from a place of deep care for them.
- **Talk about yourself.** Transition topics to one regarding your life. There may be no smooth transition here, so just jump in wherever you can! Other people might enjoy the break from their own issues, or enjoy feeling like they've supported you. Transitioning to a neutral topic you enjoy discussing—like a film that's popular, or a cause you're both passionate about—is another option to make the conversation more engaging and fun for you.
- **Remember that you aren't there to solve their problems.** Let the other person find their own answers—and validate their feelings. "It seems you are really frustrated with the way things are going at work, and you've felt that way for a long time. That must be hard." Or "Seems like this new exercise routine is really helping you feel more relaxed."
- **Remind yourself that life and relationships are cyclical.** This may be just a season with a loved one during which they are more needy. If this has been consistent behavior for a long time, being consistent with your boundaries is crucial.

- **Stay in touch with what you enjoy about the relationship.** If there are activities you love to do together or subjects you love to discuss, prioritize these to nurture the relationship.

Many times, a relationship can be rebalanced, as often the other person isn't aware that they are dominating conversations and acting self-centered. Prioritize yourself, and always feel free to pull away or create space if a relationship isn't healthy for you. Prioritizing yourself may send others a message to prioritize you too!

REBALANCE RELATIONSHIPS & AVOID ENABLING NARCISSISTIC TENDENCIES

The topic of empaths and narcissists is a popular one! Some people feel that empaths can unknowingly attract or enable those with narcissistic tendencies. An empath can easily feel that someone with narcissistic tendencies, or someone who is going through a toxically selfish and self-absorbed phase, needs to have all the attention on them all the time, needs to control the energy and emotions of the room, or needs to have the constant sympathy of others. Empaths may try to fulfill those needs for attention, control, and sympathy for many reasons, but none of them are healthy. Whether you suspect someone may be self-absorbed in general or just leaning on you too much, try the following exercise. Remember that people with deeply rooted psychological issues may not be capable of changing easily, quickly, or without professional help.

STEP 1: Relax, quiet your mind, and ask your intuition to identify a relationship in your life where the balance might be off. Is someone treating you too much like their therapist or wanting more support than you can give?

STEP 2: Notice if your intuition whispers a name or shows you a face in your mind. You might also immediately think of someone you spoke to recently, or a text might come in from someone as a synchronicity.

STEP 3: Discern if this is a season or cycle in the relationship, or if it seems to be a consistent pattern of behavior.

STEP 4: Employ tools (try to implement at least three) from the previous section to bring more balance to this relationship.

STEP 5: If you employ those tools consistently, and they do not work over time, consider your other options. Also consider if this person is displaying narcissistic tendencies. If so, they have needs you can never fulfill.

> ## MANTRA
> I love to listen and offer support to loved ones. Yet sometimes what they require is not what I can provide. Prioritizing myself, in conversations and in how I spend my time, helps keep my relationships balanced.

Establishing Rules for How You Prefer to Be Treated

So often in life we are given rules, or clear guidelines, for what is expected of us. When you enter a library, you're told to keep your voice down, and that you must return books on time. When you start elementary school as a child, you're told to play nicely and share with other children, and that you must raise your hand before you speak. When you start a job, you are usually given a clear list of duties and are trained by a supervisor. Likewise, individual people often have rules, or at least strong preferences, about how they want to be treated by others.

Being flexible with rules can be a good thing. Sometimes, in certain circumstances or with certain people, it's best to bend the rules. Empaths might be more inclined to bend the rules regarding how they prefer to be treated by others and end up doing so too often. People-pleasing means putting others' needs before your own, and in extreme cases disregarding your own needs entirely. As empaths can sense what other people are feeling and what they need so easily, it's equally easy for empaths to become very compassionate and want to bend their rules, or bend over backward, to accommodate someone else.

You might have a rule that you prefer not to be in romantic relationships with people experiencing an active addiction. Yet you then meet a magical human who is a lifelong chain smoker and begin to fall madly in love. It's easier to know when to bend your rules with someone when you are at least *aware* of your rules. Writing down your personal rules for how you prefer to be treated in relationships is, in itself, a way to anchor into your own energy. Centering and grounding into your own system and your own life is always a healthy practice for hyperperceptive empaths.

When you start to feel anxious with someone, or feel that something energetically is off with you, go back to your list of rules. Is this relationship violating any of them? If so, is this a time to bend that rule, or let the other person know this is a non-negotiable rule for you? These questions are ones you might need to sit with for hours, days, or even weeks. And you might find someone wise and neutral—like an old friend or trusted counselor—to chew on these questions with you.

When you know what you prefer in different relationships—like business, romantic, or friendship—and can communicate those preferences to others, it sets you up for much healthier, more nourishing relationships with less conflict and drama. Others may appreciate knowing how to please you and show you respect, just as you probably appreciate knowing how to please and respect the people in your life, whom you no doubt care for and value so much. Open communication about what's important to both people can really help a relationship flourish! Communicating your rules to others with love and patience, and getting curious about their rules, is a way to show how much you value the relationship and care about its success.

Writing down your rules to get clear on them, as we'll do in the next exercise, can be a helpful practice when entering a new romantic relationship or any kind of significant partnership, after a relationship breakup (including friend or business), when you're in a phase of inner-work and healing, if you're wanting to improve your confidence and self-esteem, or if you're trying to set healthier boundaries.

If you're unclear on what someone else's rules are, don't be shy about asking, like saying, "I'm getting that when you're really angry, you don't like to talk it through at first. It seems better for you to retreat, and then let me know when you're ready to talk. Is that right?" Or, "I'm sensing that you want more freedom with your schedule. To you it seems more important that the job be done and done with excellence than clocking in for a certain amount of time. I can be open to that, because what's important to me is that you really care about the quality of your work, which I can see you do."

Be sure to add some light, playful energy to your rule-setting as well. While some of your rules may sound quite serious (and that's appropriate with certain issues), others can reflect the sense of fun and joy you hope to achieve in relationships. "I value creativity in my business partnerships" or "I celebrate the unique quirks of loved ones and enjoy their eccentricity."

Sometimes a rule might be something that seems very minor, but the fact that others know it and observe it can communicate deep affection. If you have a sibling who hates ice in any drink (and has since childhood) and you remember to honor this rule even while busy setting the table for a large family gathering on a hot summer day, your sibling may look up at you and beam with affection when they sit down to the only place setting with a glass of water without ice. Allowing other people to be themselves while they allow you to do the same—in both big and small ways—is the beauty of rule-setting.

COMPILE YOUR RELATIONSHIP RULES

STEP 1: Get out paper and something to write with. Then come up with five to fifteen rules for how you prefer to be treated in a relationship. For this exercise, these should be general and apply to most relationships—whether it's a family member, friend, romantic interest, or coworker (you can also make separate, more specific lists for specific types of relationships). You may find that some of your rules are related to your empath sensitivity. Be sure to add in at least one rule that feels fun, playful, or quirky. Here are some examples of rules to get you kick-started:

I ask that people treat me with kindness and respect.

My sensitivity is something that has to be honored and understood in a general way by those I'm in a close relationship with.

I love people, but sometimes I just need my space or healthy alone time.

I prefer for people to be assertive in their communication with me.

Loving to help people is part of my nature, but I cannot rescue anyone.

I enjoy having music playing in the house on weekends and need full permission to break into dance at any moment!

STEP 2: Once you have your list of rules compiled, you might consider placing them somewhere discreet to remind yourself of them, like on the bathroom mirror at home or by a reading lamp at your bedside. Keep in mind that your rules are unique to you, and can be revised or reworded any time as your needs, desires, circumstances, relationships, or preferences change.

STEP 3: Practice communicating your rules to others, with compassion and diplomacy. Remember to treat others how you would like to be treated—this is referred to as the Golden Rule. Get curious about and observe what other people's rules might be, whether they are consciously aware of these relationship preferences or not.

> ### MANTRA
> Establishing rules in a relationship can be a loving act of caretaking, stemming from the desire for the relationship to flourish and be successful. Taking the time and energy to set boundaries in a relationship can be a reflection of how much I value the relationship.

Telling Others What You Admire About Them

While it's useful to give other people helpful feedback about stuff they may need to work on or become more aware of, it's nice to balance that by letting others know what you admire about them. Building others up is a wonderful method of nurturing your relationships and empowering other people. It's also a unique way to identify what you value in others so you might cultivate one of their character traits or embody a bit of that energy yourself!

As an energy-sensitive person, it might be easier for you to channel someone else's grace. If you admire a friend because she has a talent for meeting challenges head-on and taking charge, you might channel a bit of her "boss lady" energy when you're feeling scared and intimidated about something in your life. Likewise, if you have a colleague with a lovely soft and gentle energy, you might channel a bit of their energy when trying to be more nurturing with yourself or a child in your life.

I've found that building people up has worked wonders in my personal relationships, and it's something I always try to do with clients. A great two-step method for building others up is:

- Isolating something about this person that you admire (like their compassion) and then identifying a concrete example (like the time they didn't judge or shame you for making a mistake).
- Communicating this admiration to them clearly, like saying "Thank you for being so generous with me when I messed up last week. You could have come down hard on me like a lot of other people did, and I appreciated how compassionately you offered me gentle words of wisdom that helped me put the situation into perspective instead. Compassion is really one of your strengths."

Being overly critical and judgmental of others is a major block to more intimacy. Some people who are overly critical and judgmental of others, and have trouble accepting the messy or imperfect parts of life, were modeled this in childhood or their culture. Building up others is a nice way to shift this pattern and might be a nice way to practice building up yourself too, or a means of doing a little repair work on an important relationship in your life. It's also a great way to practice cultivating energy—which we'll do in the next exercise.

ADOPT & ADAPT SOMEONE ELSE'S INSPIRING ENERGY

STEP 1: Identify a character trait or personal grace of someone else that you'd love to adopt. It can be someone you know personally, like a neighbor, or someone you follow in the public eye.

STEP 2: Practice taking on that energy or channeling that grace, like picturing your "boss lady" friend's face before you walk into your manager's office to discuss a raise, or chatting with a coworker who has soft, gentle energy before you go home to talk to your teen employing a similar energy.

STEP 3: Notice how this energy expresses itself uniquely with you and blends with your own. In other words, *adapt* it. This is not about pretending to be someone else or something you're not. It's also not about denying your authenticity or emotions. You could feel really sad about something, for instance, but also channel a friend's natural optimism or positivity to insert some hope into the equation.

> ## MANTRA
> When I admire something about someone else, I tell them. My admiration can also be a clue that this is an energy I'd like to practice cultivating in myself.

Feeling Connected through Heart Energy

Humans crave feeling connected to others; and even though empaths can sometimes also crave healthy space from others, empaths are nourished by the heart energy created through connection. Yet there are times in our lives, or times in the world, when connecting with others can be harder to achieve.

You might have felt very isolated during the recent pandemic, for example, or you might have recently moved to a new area where you don't know anyone, or you might be going through a breakup. There are seasons when circumstances might make us feel more separate or isolated . . . yet that desire and need for human connection remains a constant.

Part of what happens when we connect with someone else is that our energetic heart comes forward so we can feel that nourishing energy of two hearts commingling—and bathe in heart energy. Our energetic hearts are activated and recharged by this type of healing connection, and our energetic hearts keep humming happily long after the connection is over. Feeling connected is one of the ways we keep our energetic heart healthy, like how you take your car for a tune-up—and then it runs better afterward!

If you're feeling lonely or disconnected, and hanging out in person with someone who makes you feel heart-warmed isn't possible, try one of the following to bathe in heart energy and feel connected:

1. **Call or have a video chat with someone.** Heart energy can travel through phones, email exchanges, and texts. Hanging out face to face with someone or a group of people can be really connecting, yet using modern technology to connect also activates heart energy!

2. **Watch a TV show that stars heart energy.** This might be a show set in a small town with a tight-knit community, where people care about each other and support each other. The show could highlight heart themes like acceptance, inclusion, forgiveness, grace, and healing.

3. **Listen to one of your favorite artists whose music is tenderhearted.** Sometimes putting on a favorite album with nurturing energy is like hanging out with an old friend.

4. **Listen to a podcast where there's a great conversation and the host magnifies a lot of heart energy,** like compassion, self-love, and

humor. Finding someone who does regular podcasts or YouTube videos whose energy is caring and service-oriented, and tuning in regularly, can be a wonderful way to feel connected.

5. **Join an online or in-person community** of people who are supportive and like-minded, like a spiritual community, a book club, a sports club, or a nature club.

6. **Volunteer your time** with someone who would be grateful for your attention and care, like walking shelter dogs, reading to children at a library, or helping out at a food pantry.

7. **Send a card or care package in the mail to someone you love.** You'll feel so connected putting it together, and the smile or thank-you from them could generate a lot of yummy heart energy!

8. **Give someone a compliment or tell someone "thank you."** This can be a great way to create connection and generate heart energy among coworkers or people you don't know as well, like new neighbors.

Heart energy is sustaining for the human spirit, and ideally we all require a daily dose. Think of it as an energy vitamin! As someone sensitive to energy, you are good at creating heart energy and absorbing it from others.

BATHE IN HEART ENERGY!

STEP 1: The next time you're feeling lonely or disconnected, and hanging out with someone special in person to activate heart energy isn't possible, come back to this section of the book to discern how you can bathe in heart energy.

STEP 2: Quiet your mind and ask your intuition for a number between 1 and 8. When you see a number as an image in your mind or hear a number as a voice in your mind, check which suggestion from the previous section matches that number. I heard "two" in my mind, which means I should watch a TV show with heart energy to feel more connected. If you didn't hear or see a number in your mind, scan the suggestions and use your clairsentient psychic pathway to discern which number has the strongest, most intriguing energy pull for you. When I tried this, I was attracted by the energy of number 8—the suggestion about giving compliments and telling people "thank you."

STEP 3: If your intuition suggested bathing in heart energy in a way that does not involve reaching out to a person you know, follow your intuition's guidance, but also reach out to someone with a call, text, etc. Suggestion numbers 1, 7, and 8 all involve reaching out to someone special you know for connection.

> ### MANTRA
> Part of why I crave spending time with others is the lovely heart energy this activates. When hanging out with special people isn't possible, there are other ways I can create a similar feeling of connection and bathe in heart energy!

Creating Healthy Space by Anchoring into Your Own Energy

Having someone else in your energy field on a regular basis can be a huge blessing. I've been married for over twenty years, and at times my husband

and I have lived in some pretty tight quarters! Currently we have a spacious home, yet we both work from home. Besides seeing each other all day, we are best friends, so we spend a ton of time together. You may have a similar situation, like a roommate, child, parent, or coworker who you value having in your life and who is in your energy field on a regular basis. While these relationships are part of what makes life so precious and magical, they may pose special challenges for some empaths.

Because empaths can feel other people's energies and emotions in their own system, this can set sensitive people up to have more issues with codependency or enmeshment. (We've already touched upon both of these terms in this book.) *Codependency* is when you are no longer independent, so your sense of safety or well-being is defined by the other person. An example would be not being able to feel happy or peaceful until the other person is feeling that way too. The American Psychological Association defines *enmeshment* as "a condition in which two or more people, typically family members, are involved in each other's activities and relationships to an excessive degree . . ."; and there may be some overlap between these two terms.

As we have covered previously in this book, when you are sensitive enough to feel what others feel, you could try to manage other people's emotions to cope. That way, if they feel good, you feel good, right? This sounds like a simple fix, but in reality it is actually much more draining— not to mention unhealthy and unrealistic. Sensitive empaths may try to manage other people's lives and emotions as a coping skill, often without realizing it.

We've already covered how witnessing and observing others is an excellent coping skill for empaths, and here we will cover another coping skill for being a sensitive person in a close relationship to someone else— anchoring into your own energy. Suggestions for this include:

▪ **Having close relationships outside a primary relationship.** Meeting a friend for lunch on Saturday while your partner does something else, taking a yoga class with an instructor you like while your kids are at school, or hanging outside the house with someone else while your roommate stays home and enjoys the space all to themselves are great examples.

- **Keeping up with interests and hobbies that you don't share with the other person.** This could look like making time to go hiking with a group even though your partner isn't a nature person, making time to host your monthly book club even though your adult child who lives with you doesn't like the same genre, or having a home altar in your bedroom even though your roommate isn't spiritual.
- **Identifying and embracing your natural style.** So what if your best friend doesn't like boho-chic clothing, or your child thinks you laugh too loud, or your roommate doesn't like Thai food? Finding ways to be in a relationship to others with respect and kindness, while still being allowed to be our authentic selves, helps prevent enmeshment.
- **Celebrating people's differences.** We are all unique pieces of a larger puzzle. Sometimes your genius is tied to what is unique or most different about you. While it's good to cooperate with others, compromise, and be flexible, a homogeneous society might not be as healthy. Try to celebrate and embrace other people's quirks and uniqueness—as well as your own.
- **Getting in touch with aspects of you that have stood the test of time.** Is there a musical artist you loved as a child . . . and still love to sing or dance along with? Perhaps you've been an activist for a certain worthy cause for decades. Or is there a talent or passion that has been part of your life for as long as you can remember, like reading fantasy novels, telling jokes, acting in plays, or running marathons? Stay in touch with the parts of yourself that reveal your true nature or may even be a glimpse into your soul.

■ **Being allowed to have space and alone time.** It's crucial that people in your life understand that sometimes, as a sensitive person, you just need space from the relationship, or healthy alone time. This is good for all humans in close relationships, and I think it can be especially helpful for empaths. Give others this same grace, communicating to each other that asking for space or alone time doesn't mean you value or love the other person any less. I was very lucky regarding this issue, as my mother taught me early how healthy and even fun getting space and alone time can be.

Codependency and enmeshment are complex issues and could have even developed as a coping skill in childhood. If you suspect they're issues for you, there's nothing wrong with you. Getting help—through support groups, counseling, and books by experts—can be amazingly useful in giving you healthier tools to manage your close relationships.

DROP ANCHOR

STEP 1: Dropping anchor into your own energy does not have to be complicated. You may not have to meditate for a long time, hold the perfect crystal, or repeat a special mantra. Simply spend time, outside one of your primary relationships, doing something you love.

STEP 2: Connect with what helps you define your identity in a healthy way—outside of your closest relationship(s). My closest relationship is with my husband. Yet I have aspects of my identity that have nothing to do with being a wife. I'm a sister, an author, a friend, an intuitive, and someone who has loved listening to Stevie Nicks since I was a child! My husband and I share a lot in common, but sometimes our taste in films, books, and music is very different.

STEP 3: Identify activities and places you enjoy that the other person doesn't. I like eating at certain restaurants, browsing certain bookstores, writing at certain coffee shops, stretching at certain yoga studios, and walking in certain parks that my husband doesn't, for example. Prioritize spending time at the places or doing the activities the other person has no interest in.

STEP 4: Remind yourself that being in relationships is messy and imperfect. None of us are getting it "right" or keeping it healthy all the time. Also, every relationship is different, and what works for every relationship will be somewhat different. Yet if someone makes you feel that being independent or spending time away from them is not okay, reach out for help and support.

> ## MANTRA
> Relationships are more fun when I have some autonomy. After all, I enjoy my own company! Having independence actually strengthens my close relationships, and knowing that I can ask for healthy space and alone time makes me feel more safe and comfortable as a sensitive person about entering new intimate relationships.

LONE WOLF OR PACK ANIMAL

This is another quiz where there are no right or wrong answers. While I believe strongly that empaths require generous amounts of space and healthy alone time, I also believe humans are pack animals and benefit enormously from being in community with others. Where you fall on the introvert/extrovert spectrum, as we covered in Chapter 1, will also influence how much alone time versus group time is nourishing for you.

I hope the questions in this quiz help you achieve that balance in your own unique way. Simply answer yes or no to the following questions.

1. I have a pack of friends, and a few of them at least know each other as acquaintances. While I enjoy one-on-one time with each of them, I sometimes schedule hang sessions with three or more people at once, which creates a different energy and its own brand of fun.

2. Professionally I like to network, and I belong to a group of colleagues that periodically gets together either in person or virtually to exchange ideas, build comradery, and share best practices.

3. As a sensitive person I can sometimes get overwhelmed by large crowds, yet this doesn't stop me from occasionally attending live concerts, sporting events, or other activities with big groups of people I don't know.

4. When I'm invited to a party or social gathering and I don't know many people there, I use this as an excuse to practice talking to new people and expand my social circle.

5. I've been getting used to the idea of online communities in this digital age, and whether it's participating in a group chat when I'm taking an online workshop or joining a Facebook group, I'm finding ways to make online communities work for me and help me feel more connected with like-minded people.

6. Family is something I define for myself. I have a group of very close, long-term friends and colleagues who are like family, and I also have people I'm related to whom I can bond with. It's important for me to stay close with all these people and make time for these relationships.

7. My community is something I'm involved in, whether I buy from local shops, support local children's charities, volunteer my time to a local organization, or cast my vote on important local issues.

8. At times in my life, I've been in therapy or reached out for support in group settings. Whether it was/is a group of recovering addicts, a group of people healing from a similar trauma, or a group of people pursuing a similar health goal, I have found the group dynamic uniquely supportive.

9. I love to learn, and I enjoy taking classes or workshops in a group setting. It might last for an afternoon, a weekend, several months, or even several years, but I believe there is something to be gained by educational models based on group settings.

10. I'm part of a spiritual community that meets regularly. Even when I don't always interact with other members directly, just seeing their faces and smiles, or just knowing their energy is present online, makes me feel connected.

ANSWERED MOSTLY NO:

You may be a lone wolf who is looking for their pack. As some-one who's a bit of a hermit (sitting around writing books, calendars, and oracle decks alone all day kind of demands it), I can relate. There may be contributing factors or tem-porary circumstances regarding why you answered mostly no. You may experience social anxiety, you may be triggered by crowds or large groups whether in-person or online, you may be brand-new to an area where you live, or you may be going through a transition where you've outgrown a lot of your old relationships. Whatever your situation, remind your-self that there are tools to help you navigate group dynamics as a sensitive person. Reach out for those tools and support. There's something magical about group energy, and any group would benefit so much from your presence!

ANSWERED MOSTLY YES:

I'm so happy to learn that you have such supportive com-munity in your life. As an empath, also make sure to priori-tize healthy alone time. Sometimes empaths who are part of many groups, like a busy working parent (you might be part of an office, a larger family structure, a group of parents at school, etc.), might get used to going without healthy alone time. Even if you can go without it, and have become condi-tioned to go without it, remind yourself that you still benefit enormously from healthy alone time. It not only enhances your ability to connect with your sensitivity and intuition, healthy alone time also helps you decompress when you are overstimulated by the energies, emotions, and physi-cal stimuli outside yourself. Above all, healthy alone time centers you, and from that place you are more clear and commanding. If your cup runneth over regarding the bless-ing of community, you may just need to be strategic about how you prioritize healthy alone time.

Chapter 5

Your Empath Heart and Your Relationship with the World

We might not think of it in these terms, but each of us has our own unique relationship to the larger world. How we are of service, how we approach suffering in the world, and how we stay connected to ourselves while being part of a larger whole are topics covered in this chapter.

I've always been someone who liked knowing what was happening in the world, probably because I find the journey of other people, and the stories of their lives, fascinating. And, like most people, I want to help alleviate suffering. From a young age I was passionate about certain causes and global issues, and history was always one of my favorite subjects in school growing up. Whatever the year is when you happen to be reading this book, you are part of the history of that time. And even though you are just one empath, you, like every human, have an important role to play.

Being sensitive to collective energy as an empath, it may be easy for you to resonate with the spiritual idea that we are all connected. In the Internet age, and with our current global crises as I write this book in 2022, perhaps our collective connection is more apparent than ever. For the very compassionate heart, what happens to one person can resonate out, like how plucking one string on a harp will cause the others to vibrate. This world is really one instrument, which we are all forever striving to play more harmoniously.

I hope this chapter helps you navigate the magical, mystical relationship you have to the larger world in practical, grounded, service-oriented ways.

Enjoying Empath Community

After an intuitive session recently with a new client, my client told me, "It was so nice to just talk to someone about intuition and sensitivity who understands. I've been craving that kind of connection lately." Reading a book like this one can be a delightful way to normalize your empath experience and feel empowered. And it can also be nice to have people in your life who just get it, like other sensitives.

It was a friend—many, many years ago—who first told me I was "sensitive." I knew I was very intuitive, but I wasn't as familiar with the concept of sensitivity at the time. This friend has become a special reminder and a trusted resource regarding sensitivity over the years, because she just gets it. She's the sort of friend who is aware of her sensitivity and curious about it, so we can compare notes for what works and doesn't work for us as empaths—as far as managing and maximizing sensitivity. Sometimes what works for one of us won't work for the other, and vice versa.

You might find a coworker who is also sensitive and open to the concept, or you might follow someone in the public eye who embodies sensitivity. Today there are many authors, podcasters, health-care professionals, and YouTubers who identify as empaths or as sensitives and love to share information or create community among sensitive people.

I have many beloved friends, family members, and colleagues who are either not as sensitive as I am, or simply aren't interested in or don't resonate with this concept. I really value and enjoy these people and their perspectives. Yet I also find it helpful to have some people in my personal life, and some folks I follow in the public eye, who just get it as far as sensitivity goes.

SEEK OUT OTHER SENSITIVES

STEP 1: Ask your intuition who in your life is also sensitive and might be open to bonding over your shared sensitivity. Quiet your mind and relax. Do you see a face in your mind, hear a name in your mind, or have a breakthrough thought about someone? You might get the intuitive hit the next time you interact with a sensitive person, feeling physical or energetic clues from your clairsentient psychic pathway.

STEP 2: Is there someone in the public eye you follow because they are also sensitive? This may be a concept they talk about in language that resonates with you, using terms such as empathy, intuition, or sensitivity. Or they may focus on topics that are often of interest to sensitive people.

STEP 3: The next time you have a question about something regarding your sensitivity, or want help managing or maximizing it, recall the folks you identified in this exercise. Seek them out for assistance, support, and comradery.

> ## MANTRA
> Connecting with other sensitive people can inform my empath journey, making it so much more enjoyable and rewarding!

Loving Yourself to Heal Overgiving

Being so sensitive to others' emotional experience can make some empaths very compassionate, which can lead to overgiving. As a general rule, when you are depleting yourself to prioritize someone else, that's overgiving. There are certain situations or seasons where overgiving is a necessity . . . just ask the parent of a newborn if they feel depleted! However, no matter what season you are in or what your life circumstances are, it's best to minimize overgiving as much as possible.

You may never have had an issue with overgiving, or you may be an overgiver in recovery. If you struggle to set internal and external boundaries about giving, approaching your self-love practice in a new way may help. To people who love to give, and can sometimes get the balance off and overgive, prioritizing themselves might seem a little selfish. Yet there is nothing selfish about self-love.

Every year, I write a bestselling page-a-day calendar called *A Year of Self-Love*; and I also wrote a book about self-love, *Love Notes to My Self.* While working on these projects, and working on my own self-love practice, I realized that loving, valuing, and supporting oneself actually makes you more compassionate toward other people! It's true that when you prioritize your own self-care in a loving way, you naturally have more physical stamina and emotional reserves to show up for others. Yet there's more to it—an energy component; and as an empath, I know that's something you'll be interested in and intrigued by!

When my work began to expand into the arena of self-love, starting to write, think, and teach about self-love made me practice it more in my daily life. I found that being more compassionate and gentle with myself in my thoughts and actions actually made me feel and act much more compassionately and gently toward other people. What I realized was that by holding an energy of compassion and gentleness with myself—in my own energetic core, where we are each most powerful—I was able to generate so much more compassion in general. My heart energy was more online and present. Compassion was an energy I was creating; and aligning with that was actually easier to hold and sustain because that compassion began and ended with me each day. Like a well-worn path in a forest, or a well-developed neural pathway in the brain, compassion became easy and natural for me to slide into. It became my default operating mode.

Naturally, I still got angry at people and got into arguments with people. That's actually healthy, especially if we can hold a certain level of compassion for ourselves, and the general world, in the process.

If you are someone who always worries about friends and family, or whose heart always goes out to the people suffering the most in the world, know that prioritizing yourself and your own self-love practice will make you an even stronger force of compassion in the world. You can achieve this without overgiving, since when you feel depleted, what you are giving is watered down. You also open yourself up to burnout when you overgive, which may shut you down temporarily from being able to give at all while you recover.

You can hold a gentle energy with yourself while still setting boundaries with others and yourself, and while holding others and yourself accountable. Opening up to more compassion with yourself and others does not mean you have to become a doormat or ignore self-discipline. Give yourself permission to love yourself, and treat yourself as well as possible! It's not selfish. When done mindfully, it has the opposite energetic effect.

PRIORITIZE YOUR OWN HAPPINESS

STEP 1: Make the mindful decision to prioritize your own happiness. This can feel revolutionary and be a game-changer if you struggle with people-pleasing. As you prioritize your own happiness in big and small ways, trust that the people who love you and truly want the best for you will want to remain in your life as you begin showing up to life in a new way.

STEP 2: Start small, like telling a neighbor "no" when they ask you for another favor, or saying "no" to a work collaboration. Then say "yes" to something you do want to do—like rest, work on a creative hobby, attend a class, or spend time with a family member. As you are compassionate with yourself by prioritizing your own happiness, notice if this makes you treat others with more compassion, even when you have to tell them "no."

STEP 3: Think big, and consider something larger that would make you happy, like going back to school, committing to a relationship or separating from someone, starting a side hustle, or volunteering for a cause close to your heart. Contemplate this bigger change and how it might affect others. Talk it through with safe, supportive people and ask yourself how you might start slowly moving toward this big change with compassion for yourself and others.

STEP 4: *Don't* ignore your responsibilities. We are all interdependent on each other, so sometimes we need to show up for a loved one, or show up for a shift at work, when we really don't feel like it. Ignoring our obligation might make us feel happier in the short-term, yet maybe not in the long-term. *Do* investigate if you could honor your responsibilities in a way that would bring you more happiness.

STEP 5: As you prioritize your own happiness, ask yourself where and when you might have seen martyrdom modeled, and if martyrdom holds any benefits to you. For example, you might have had a parent or guardian who was often a martyr to other people's happiness, needs, and desires. You might realize that subconsciously you believe that being a martyr keeps people from leaving, keeps others loving you, or somehow keeps you safe. Childhood issues, like not being valued enough by wounded caregivers, might have left you with a subconscious lack of self-worth. Remind yourself how valuable you are, and that your happiness is important! Look at this issue with curiosity and healthy emotional detachment, and let the wisdom naturally follow.

> ## MANTRA
> How we treat others can sometimes be a reflection of how we treat ourselves. Having more compassion for myself may help me have more compassion to share with the world.

Being of Service

Every client who has come to me for an intuitive session is amazingly unique. Yet after doing so many readings on people from all over the world and all walks of life, it's equally amazing how similar people's concerns can be. One of the most common questions people want to discuss in a reading with me is: "Why am I here—what should I be doing with my life?"

Intuitive information can come to me during a session that a client has a talent for teaching, guiding, healing, protecting, nurturing, leading, creating, building, communicating, or networking. Yet these natural talents can express themselves in many ways. We have all been handed a coffee or tea from a very *nurturing* barista, who becomes a go-to person to get a pick-me-up drink from and chat with because their energy starts our day off right. Or you might have encountered a financial professional who helped in *healing* some of your money issues by getting your taxes in order or teaching you about investment best practices. Or you might work in a busy office where you're not technically a manager, yet you always end up *teaching* new hires all about office culture and company protocols.

Humans long to be of service, which can give their life an even richer sense of purpose, joy, or meaning. The way you're of service can evolve throughout your life. As a child, I wanted to be a teacher or a psychologist. As I got into college, that changed, and I dreamed of being a writer. Then after working at magazines and newspapers in my twenties (and writing a novel that never got published), I found myself wanting to work for a nonprofit in my thirties and help people who were struggling. In my early forties, I started giving intuitive readings and writing nonfiction books. I'm open to my service evolving in my fifties.

Sometimes, how we are of service has nothing to do with a job. You might be a volunteer. Or you might have an animal or young person or partner you show up for every day. Or you might wake up every morning with the intention of being an ambassador of kindness to anyone you encounter throughout the day. Being of service is simply and profoundly the fundamental desire to offer support to others.

For empaths who are wired to connect so intimately with other people, the connection created by supporting someone else could be particularly nourishing for you. As an empath, you can feel, in your own system, the gratitude someone else feels toward you for your support. All you need to do to experience that wonderful energy exchange as a sensitive person is to be *present* while supporting others.

If your current roles or relationships don't provide that sense of connection, purpose, joy, or meaning, it might be about making a change: that change could look like exploring your options, or showing up in your current roles and relationships with more presence and a different attitude or outlook. Like anyone else, as an empath you can go through periods of burnout or illness where it's not about supporting others as much as getting more support for yourself. Many times, life is a balance of offering support to others and seeking out support for yourself.

Even people who have experienced devastating loss can often inspire us by the ways they find to keep being of service. As a writer, I'm always intensely inspired by Jean-Dominique Bauby, author of *The Diving Bell and the Butterfly*. After he had a seizure, Bauby experienced locked-in syndrome: his mental faculties were intact, but he could not speak or move, except for the ability to blink one eyelid. Before his seizure, he was the editor of French *Elle* magazine, and had signed a contract to write a book, which he was very excited about. After his seizure, he dictated the book by blinking out each letter of each word to an editor (known as the silent alphabet). Two days after the book was published, he passed away following a bout with pneumonia.

Many, many times I have been on a very tight deadline for a book, and thought with wonder and pride, as a fellow human, of this man's accomplishment. His feat was truly phenomenal, and he has been of service to people like me who he inspires by example. You might volunteer at a community garden or plant a tree in your neighborhood, and never know the joy your effort continues to give to so many for years after you've gone. Being kind to a stranger you interact with on the phone or at a store could be a nourishing encounter that lifts their spirit for days. In the next exercise, we'll practice being more present when you're offering or accepting support, so you can feel more of the nourishing energy exchange.

FEEL MORE PRESENT WHILE
BEING OF SERVICE

STEP 1: The next time you find yourself supporting and being of service to someone else—at home, at work, or by coincidence in the world—practice being more present in the moment. If you're craving being of service, look for ways to make someone else's day in small yet meaningful ways, and stay present as you do.

STEP 2: Notice what you're experiencing with your five physical senses any time you want to feel more present, like the smile on someone else's face or the sound of their "thank you." Be more present in general to what you're seeing, hearing, tasting, touching, or smelling while being of service. For example, notice the smell of the soup you prepare for a child, or the unique look of someone else's haircut as they walk into your clothing store to browse.

STEP 3: Assign meaning to your offering. If you work construction, for example, you might walk away from the job site each day reminding yourself that the house you're building will be a dream come true for the new owner, and may even be passed down to other generations in that family. If you deliver packages, imagine how grateful the person will feel who opens their door and sees it there waiting.

STEP 4: When someone is supporting you, practice presence by remembering to thank them or give them a compliment on their work. One issue that stops us from being more present in the moment is racing thoughts. You could leave a doctor's appointment and realize you wished you'd thanked the nurse who helped you, but you had a million other things on your mind.

When you're offering or accepting support, use it as practice to be more present in the moment by quieting your mind and gently focusing on what's in front of you.

My brand-new dryer stopped working recently, and even after a month of the repair people coming out to look at it, no one knew what to do. Finally, the company sent their most experienced repair person, who told me he was determined to figure out the issue. He did, within a few hours! It felt like a mini-miracle. When I told him in a gushing way how thankful I was and gave him a cash tip, he was beaming. It felt so good to see that smile and pride on his face, and know that I helped him remember how much his work is appreciated.

> **MANTRA**
>
> When I'm wanting to be of greater service, it can indicate a pivotal moment in my career or relationships or volunteer work, or it could mean being more present to all the ways life already gives me the chance to be of service.

Making Intentional Money Decisions

We may like it, or we may not, but money is an integral part of life and affects many of our relationships. It could be argued that your relationship to money itself is one of your primary, foundational relationships. For empaths who can feel what others want so easily, it may be easy to be swayed by others about how to handle your money.

Ten years ago I was on a trip to Boulder, Colorado, browsing in a store that sold crystals, when I overheard a woman buying a huge crystal that cost thousands of dollars. The clerk in that shop was very nice and charming, and had been chatting to me earlier, explaining the properties of various crystal specimens. We even started chatting about other subjects, and were really enjoying each other's company. But once it became clear that the other woman in the shop was going to buy one of the *really expensive* crystals and I wasn't, that customer understandably got the clerk's full attention.

The clerk nodded and smiled at me while listening to the other customer talk as they finalized the sale. I really appreciated that nod and smile—the clerk was able to communicate to me very quickly that they'd enjoyed chatting with me. I knew the clerk needed to prioritize the larger sale over helping me decide on a forty-five-dollar crystal! Meanwhile, trying to decide between two very large, expensive crystals, the other customer told the clerk with a sigh, "Well, it doesn't matter which one I buy. My daughter will end up with it anyway. She seems to end up with all my pretty things." The customer and clerk laughed to lighten the energy.

What an interesting scene, I thought at the time. So many money decisions were being played out in the shop that day. My decision about sticking to my budget, the woman's decision about making a bigger purchase, the clerk's decision about which customer to prioritize, and the other customer's sense that even after the clerk wrapped up this prize for her, she would probably make the decision to give the crystal away somewhat reluctantly. If the woman buying the larger crystal was sensitive, she could no doubt also feel in her own system how much the clerk naturally wanted the sale to go through.

Perhaps that other customer *was* sensitive, which is why she ended up giving things away that she preferred to keep—because as a sensitive person she could sense how much people she cared about wanted and would enjoy those pretty things. Perhaps the clerk was sensitive too, and honored that by making sure to catch my eye and give me a warm smile and acknowledging nod even though she had to shift her focus to a higher-price sale. If we assume that both the clerk and the other customer were equally sensitive, which one displayed healthier money boundaries?

As an empath, it can be dangerous to allow the desires of others to overly influence you regarding your finances, or let others dictate your financial decisions simply because you can feel the other person's feelings. It might seem prudent to make them happy so you don't have to sit in uncomfortable energy today, yet the best money decisions are often made when we consider the long-term repercussions. You might have general health goals, career goals, and relationship goals. Money goals, like goals in other areas of your life, you may hold loosely (it's not necessarily about hitting an exact dollar amount in your annual income or savings account), yet these goals give you a way to set priorities.

Regularly touching in with your money priorities is a wonderful way to anchor into your own energy regarding your finances. That way, if your partner says they want to make a big purchase, you come to the conversation centered in your current goal to increase the family savings. It may be best to be flexible and agree with your partner, but you can do that with more peace of mind by knowing your current money priorities.

On that day in Boulder at the crystal shop, it was a priority for me to get a few souvenirs to take home to remember my trip. I planned to spend some money when I walked into that shop, and was excited to do so. I would have personally liked to buy a bigger crystal to take home, and I would have liked to continue to have the clerk's full attention so we could keep our interesting chat going. I even would have really enjoyed making that clerk happy and giving them a huge day of sales on beautiful products. During our chat, the clerk mentioned they were new to the shop, still learning about crystals themselves, and felt blessed to have gotten the position. It would have made the clerk look impressive to the owner and given them a hefty commission if I had bought a large crystal too.

Yet when I walked out of the store with my forty-five-dollar crystal, I wasn't anxious about checking my bank balance, or anxious that I'd already blown my whole budget for the trip on my first afternoon. I was able to be present in the moment, relaxed, and enjoy the rest of the day with family and friends—and that was priceless.

SET PRIORITIES WITH MONEY

STEP 1: The next time you're doing something with money—like paying bills, checking your bank balance, or pondering an investment or big purchase—connect with yourself about your money priorities. You might want to buy a home, and saving for the down payment is a top priority; or you might have gotten a big windfall and want to splurge on yourself; or you might be wanting to understand your investments or Social Security benefits more as you age; or you might be a young adult starting out, and learning about monetary best practices is a high priority; or you could be recovering from something financially devastating, and regrouping and healing are the ultimate priority. Remember that you can have several different money priorities at the same time.

STEP 2: Rate your money priorities from most to least important on a piece of paper or sticky note you can save somewhere. If you have three main money priorities now, it doesn't mean that number three isn't important: it simply means that the money priority you rated as number one is the most important. Use your intuition to help you discern which money priorities are most important. A few of them might turn out to be equally important. It might be really important for you to spend money honoring your desire to go back to school and change your career, yet also important for you to limit the amount of debt you accumulate.

STEP 3: The next time you're making a money decision and feeling uncertain, consult your list of money priorities.

Get used to discerning—and then filing away as helpful knowledge—the different attitudes toward money that friends, family, and coworkers hold. Once you know someone's attitude toward money and their money priorities, and have a rough estimate of their financial history and current situation, it's much easier to separate yourself from—and put into perspective—their financial advice and wishes.

People who are not financial professionals often give money advice based on their own current situation and past financial history. So the wealthy friend who also grew up with a lot of financial abundance might encourage you to *splurge* to celebrate your recent promotion, while another friend who grew up in a poorer household and is now a big saver encourages you to *save* your promotion money to celebrate yourself. Perhaps you decide to do a little bit of both—splurge *and* save. First, you'll check your list of money priorities!

> **MANTRA**
> Part of having a healthier relationship with money is getting clear on my own financial priorities, remembering that friends, family, and colleagues will have different attitudes toward, histories with, and priorities about money.

Not Staying Frozen by Suffering in the World

There's an incomprehensible amount of suffering in the world—whether it's suffering that's distant from you, like a refugee camp or natural disaster in a far-off land, or suffering that's closer to home, like a family member with a terminal diagnosis or a friend who is desperately lonely. The sheer enormity of suffering in the world on a daily basis can be immobilizing for compassionate people, whether they are also sensitive empaths or not. As an empath who can feel collective energy—sometimes even feeling it without reading a newspaper article or hearing about what a loved one is going through—collective suffering may sometimes make you feel frozen and powerless.

If this happens to you, these steps might help:

- **Prioritize your own self-care.** This also means prioritizing your own mental and emotional health. Prioritizing your own self-care always gives you more stamina to show up for others.

- **Pull back a little from exposing yourself to suffering that's not directly related to you.** I like to stay up to date on news and the state of the world. But there are days when I can only read the headlines, and going deeper isn't the best emotional or mental-health choice for me. Everyone will have a different threshold for this, so learn your own. This threshold can fluctuate as well, based on your own current life circumstances.

- **Offer TLC to loved ones who are suffering, emphasizing quality over quantity.** One phone call when you can be really present and supportive with a loved one might be better than three calls when you are feeling burned-out and not really present. Sometimes just a quick text letting someone know you've been really busy but wanted to reach out and tell them you care can mean the world.

- **Look for ways you can help.** Whether it's making a small monthly donation to a charity or helping someone that Spirit seems to have put in your path for a reason, making a positive difference in the world will give you back a healthy sense of control, empowerment, and comfort.

- **Don't minimize your own suffering.** I've noticed that very compassionate empaths can at times downplay their own troubles because they are not "as bad" as what other people are going through. It's important to put your suffering in larger perspective—this can even make you feel more gratitude about your life, or make you feel comforted that you are not alone in suffering. Yet even when others are suffering in extreme ways, that does not invalidate your own painful experiences and emotions.

- **Create balance by exposing yourself to positive things happening in the world too.** Make sure you're also searching out stories of people watching their dreams come true. I tuned in to the end of the Super Bowl the other night just to listen to the interviews from players on the winning team. Most of these players have been working toward this win their whole lives, and I watched a player take off his helmet and, with tears in his eyes, tell the interviewer "I've dreamed of this moment! I saw it!" (A premonition?) He shook his head in disbelief as the air behind him filled with confetti and cheers. What a wonderful collective moment to share in!

- **Remind yourself that you cannot help everyone, or end all suffering.** It would be impossible for you to help everyone in the world who is suffering, so carrying that burden emotionally and energetically is impractical, as it stops you from helping those you can. Focus on how, where, when, and who you can make a difference for. This will pivot your perspective when you're feeling frozen and make you want to re-engage with the more difficult aspects of life again.

- **Practice mindful heartache.** Suffering is heartbreaking, and sometimes it's healing to open up and feel the collective suffering mindfully. If a war on the other side of the world is tugging at your heart, mindfully open up and let your heart ache with others. In some way energetically, those other people are then not going through their suffering alone. Knowing that others care, even if what they can do to help is limited, can be sustaining for people in situations of prolonged stress. Find someone else who is also concerned and experiencing heartache over this collective situation, and share what you are feeling. Hearing that other compassionate people care about suffering in the world too, and sharing a meaningful moment of eye contact or even a hug, can be very soothing.

Letting our heart ache over pain in the collective is part of how we stay connected to our humanity. For sensitive people, and all humans, we must each find our own way to accomplish this individually that is balanced and therefore *sustainable*. Our compassion demands that, so we can stay not frozen but an active force of grace in the world. .

UNFREEZE YOUR NERVOUS SYSTEM

STEP 1: Recognize when you feel frozen, powerless, or immobilized by the amount of suffering in the world. Acknowledge to yourself that, as a sensitive person, this can sometimes happen.

STEP 2: Disengage in a healthy way. This may mean avoiding certain news stories for a few days or asking for support if you're a caregiver so you can tend to yourself. Your sensitive system is overstimulated, so lower the stimulation in your environment, especially as it relates to this issue.

STEP 3: Cocoon in healthy ways, like watching your favorite heart-warming movie where characters overcome obstacles and help each other; or reading a book by your favorite positive, inspirational author; or listening to your favorite calming, feel-good album.

STEP 4: Expose yourself to some positive, celebratory energy in the world. It's not a way to deny suffering, but a way to balance the energy so you have more stamina for the suffering of yourself and others. Occasionally I'll go listen to people give emotional acceptance speeches at awards shows, or watch an athlete or singer nail a live performance victoriously, or read about a group of people celebrating a hard-won, emotional victory from another time in history.

STEP 5: Check in with yourself periodically to see if your system is recovering. If you are gradually feeling a higher tolerance for—and less overwhelmed by—suffering, that's an encouraging sign as far as recovery goes. If being exposed to suffering in the world or in your immediate circle is still really triggering days or weeks later, reach out to a health-care professional like a counselor or schedule a tune-up visit with your doctor. Keep prioritizing your own self-care, and take everything at your own pace, always and no matter what!

> **MANTRA**
> The enormous suffering in the world is real, and so is my sensitivity to it. Prioritizing my own self-care, while helping when, where, how, and who I can, helps me stay in balance and remain an active force of grace in the world.

Engaging in Sacred Activism

The ability to intimately feel the suffering of others can turn empaths into passionate change-makers in the world. Finding a cause that speaks to your empath heart and peacefully advocating for a group of people, animals, or the planet, can be a powerful way to practice being more assertive. Sometimes in life it's easier to find your courage and determination when you're not focused on just yourself. Yet that assertiveness you tap into inside through activism can positively carry over to other areas of your life, like when you're advocating for *you*—an equally important and noble cause!

Look for a cause in the larger world that means something to you personally but will also make life better for lots of other souls collectively. This, in my opinion, is the sacred and greater purpose of sensitive people on the planet. Being easily moved by the plight of others helps you care in a unique way that—when empaths band together—can move mountains for the collective good.

Empaths can easily tune into collective energy, and sometimes that's a very nourishing experience! Empaths are often encouraged to protect themselves from collective energy; but at times you may benefit more from opening yourself to it. Tapping into a peaceful social movement meant to help the world evolve into a more loving, fair place for all—fueled by the compassionate energy of many—can be an inspiring, uplifting energy wave to ride.

FIND A CAUSE

STEP 1: Identify a cause that moves your empath heart—a change you want to see in the world not only for yourself but because it will improve the lives of many.

STEP 2: Ask yourself "How can I help?" Could you donate your time, money, talent, or other resources? Could you help educate people about this cause, or learn more about it yourself?

STEP 3: Stay in touch with your mental and emotional health whenever engaging in sacred activism. Always prioritize your own well-being! If participating is making you anxious, drained, or otherwise overwhelmed, re-evaluate your level of involvement—or pull back entirely for a bit.

> **MANTRA**
> I want the world to be a kinder, more loving place for everyone, so I find ways to do my part.

Being in the Flow with Earth & Astrological Cycles

The earth and the stars have their own energy and energetic cycles, which humans have been tracking for thousands of years. There can be a palpable mood shift between different seasons—like the fresh, playful energy of spring and the focused, determined energy of fall. Where you live, what the climate is like at different times of the year there, and what the main industries are in your area can greatly influence how you, and your community collectively, experience the changing seasons.

Astrology is the ancient, evolving study of heavenly bodies, regarding how their transits might influence the collective energy, as well as individuals on Earth, that has become very popular in the modern era. Noting astrological cycles like Mercury retrograde and the phases of the moon (such as full, new, waxing, and waning) has become more common in pop culture, and may be a sign of our collective humanity having an increased sensitivity in general and thus expressing curiosity about these energy shifts.

Now that I'm older and know more about astrology, I often look back at pivotal times in my life and think: "I wonder what was going on with the planets then." It's phenomenal how sometimes what's going on in the heavens is also going on in your own life. For example, when a planet like Venus, considered among other things to rule love, goes retrograde, you might find that you're naturally re-evaluating or doing a little healing work on some of your intimate relationships.

The study of subjects like astrology can easily be a lifetime's work. And for those who enjoy delving into the intricate layers of meaning contained in a single human's astrological chart, or in the astrological chart of a single day of the year, astrology can be a lifetime's passion. For others, it might be fun to jump in where and when you can.

Anytime sensitive people pay more attention to the energy cycles that affect the planet or their corner of it, it's a way to open up to your natural connection with collective energy. That could look like spending time in nature to enjoy each season, engaging in activities associated with each season, or doing a ritual around or participating in a celebration of the changing seasons. Play with it, allowing your observations of how these cycles affect you—or how you can harness or abide by some of that shifting energy—to be one more fascinating way to explore your sensitivity!

ALIGN WITH THE ASTROLOGY OF OTHERS

STEP 1: Please approach this exercise with playful energy, not to be confused with information that prohibits you from getting along with someone or having them in your life based on their astrological chart. Every astrological sign represents archetypal energies that naturally have positive and challenging aspects—and every person is unique in how they might embody a particular sign. There's something to be learned from and celebrated about every sign! For this exercise, first pick someone you'd like to look at through an astrological lens.

STEP 2: Find out a little more about them by looking through the lens of their Sun sign. All you need to know in order to learn this is their birth date . . . you don't even have to ask them the year they were born. If you want to look at other layers, ask them the year they were born, and if they know the time of day and location. This would allow you to get access to their whole chart, including layers like their Moon sign, rising, and what sign their Venus, Mars, and Mercury are in. You can get information on your chart or someone else's for free at AstroStyle.com. The twin sisters and astrologers who run this site are a wealth of information, so poke around a bit while you're there or go to @astrotwins to follow them on Instagram.

STEP 3: While each astrologer may have their own unique opinion about the layers of a chart, they seem to all agree that the astrological sign the Sun was in when you were born is of especially significant importance. Once you determine the other person's Sun sign, try engaging with them using the following energy for fun:

- **Aries:** Engage your warrior energy, which means the Aries in your life might appreciate proactive approaches, displays of strength and resiliency, and an optimistic, can-do attitude. *Picture them as a gender-neutral knight in shining armor on a noble mission, who was the first to answer the call for assistance.*

- **Taurus:** Engage your grounded energy, which means the Taurus in your life might value stability, enjoy nature and Earth's sensual pleasures, and admire your ability to stand your ground on an issue. *Picture them as the gentle friend who offers practical advice, as well as a pint of organic ice cream in your favorite flavor, when you need support.*

- **Gemini:** Engage your communicator energy, which means the Gemini in your life might enjoy quick-witted banter, interesting and in-depth conversations where knowledge is gained, and the stimulation that comes with being a social butterfly. *Imagine them as the high-energy colleague who comes to every meeting with new information to share—while simultaneously posting masterfully about their side hustle on the latest cool social media platform.*

- **Cancer:** Engage your nurturing energy, which means the Cancer in your life may prioritize a cozy home, the comforts of good food, and a concern for their own emotions and protection as well as the emotions and protection of their loved ones. *Picture them as the strong, loyal head of a family or friend group, waiting by the hearth, fire roaring and soothing drink ready, excited to cuddle and have a heart-to-heart chat.*

- **Leo:** Engage your creative energy, which means the Leo in your life might delight in creative pursuits of all kinds, playfulness in general, and the ability to captivate others by claiming center stage. *Imagine a diva, who is a brave leader in her industry, unveiling her latest act on*

Broadway to a sold-out crowd, and for her third encore she brings a chorus of small children out to dance and sing as her adorable, silly backup band.

- **Virgo:** Engage your healer energy, which means the Virgo in your life may admire an ability to be of service to others, value detailed and practical knowledge, and crave structure and order. *Picture going to a healer whose office is clean and tidy, who listens seriously and attentively while you explain your various issues, and then presents you with an impressive action plan for how they can systematically address each one.*

- **Libra:** Engage your lover energy, which means the Libra in your life will appreciate close relationships, art, fairness and equality, and beauty. Imagine a romantic partner who loves to spend quality time with you, gets VIP tickets to the latest museum exhibit, and then wants to stare into your eyes over coffee afterward while you discuss what you just saw.

- **Scorpio:** Engage your explorer energy, which means the Scorpio in your life could want to uncover the deeper impulses and layered meanings within aspects of the human journey like sex, death, power, and money. *Imagine a masterful therapist who encourages you to examine your shadow, helps you understand your family dynamics, and helps you heal self-sabotaging patterns in your habits.*

- **Sagittarius:** Engage your philosopher energy, which means the Sagittarius in your life might wish to ponder universal truths and spiritual wisdom, the traditions of other places and cultures, and how they can remain always and forever the autonomous, free spirit. *Imagine the no-filter professor who drops bits of obscure, revelatory wisdom into conversation randomly and encourages students to view life as a fascinating adventure to be lived to the fullest!*

- **Capricorn:** Engage your achiever energy, which means the Capricorn in your life may value hard work and focused effort, consistently surmounting obstacles, and a command of Earthly authority and influence. *Picture a CEO who seems to thrive on the pressure of a packed schedule and displays an aptitude for overseeing lots of moving parts.*

- **Aquarius:** Engage your activist energy, which means the Aquarius in your life may value thinking outside the box and marching to the beat of their own drum, celebrating anything quirky or eccentric, and always taking a progressive approach. *Picture a peaceful protestor in a zany outfit who goes home afterward to unwind with the latest film from their favorite avant-garde director.*

- **Pisces:** Engage your mystic energy, which means the Pisces in your life may find comfort in the idea that we are all connected, being compassionate toward others, and the very real yet unseen world of energy. *Imagine a tarot reader with soulful eyes who draws cards for you, carefully explains your calling in this lifetime, and gives you a goodbye hug after the reading ends.*

STEP 4: If you want to relate more to this person's astrological chart, find out what their Moon sign is, or what their ascendant is, or which house a planet is in. They might have a predominant element in their chart, like fire, water, air, or earth; or a predominance of mutable, fixed, or cardinal signs. We are each an interesting celestial cocktail through the eyes of astrology!

MANTRA

Astrology is the fascinating art of mapping human archetypes. It's fun to look at the astrology of people I'm in relationship with and notice if this helps me better understand their drives and desires.

Making Your Self-Care Sacred

There are so many ways for empaths to protect themselves from unwanted energy. Just the other day I was in a session with a new client discussing her future at a big company. She described to me how after she was initially hired, her direct manager at her company began being very demanding. This manager's energy was incredibly distracting. "I'm so sorry to hear that," I told the client. "Although when I tune in to this issue with my intuition, I'm getting that this is significantly better lately. It's almost as if this manager's energy has faded to the background for you, and you aren't as bothered now."

"That's true!" the client confirmed. "I got your book *Angel Intuition*, and after reading it I asked my angels to help with this manager. But I'm not sure if they were able to do anything."

Then I saw a clairvoyant vision in my mind of an angel putting up an energy shield around my client. Part of the reason my client was now able to shrug off this manager's sometimes-annoying energy was because of the angelic energy shield.

While I will sometimes recommend things like black tourmaline, a stone that can ward off unwanted negative energy, to clients, or a client might come up with an energy-shielding technique they like to use, my go-to for all clients to aid general protection as a sensitive person is self-care. It's my gold standard for strengthening your defenses as an empath walking around in the world.

I wrote a whole book on self-care practices specifically tailored to sensitive people—*Self-Care for Empaths*—yet what works wonders are the basics: eating well, getting enough rest, moderate exercise, lowering your stress levels, and taking any supplements or medications you need.

While my client got help putting up an energy shield from the angels she called upon, as a human you naturally have an energy shield that's operating all the time—whether you realize it or not. If you love science fiction movies, you know the captain of a spaceship will often order "Shields up!" to the crew when an unidentified ship pops up on the radar. For humans, your shields are always up. However, your own self-care influences how strong and sturdy those shields are.

If you're recovering from an injury, or in the midst of a long healing journey physically or emotionally or both, remember that you still have your natural energy shield! Yet self-care becomes even more essential. Feel free to call on any benevolent spiritual force, like my client did, to help shore up your natural energy shield (Archangel Michael is my go-to).

You may notice that when you feel run-down or frazzled, it's much easier for you to be overwhelmed by the energy of the world or be pulled into distracting or negative energy that you would rather avoid. That unwelcome energy will then only further drain or frazzle you. When you realize you're in this cycle, always pivot and focus more on your self-care.

Making your self-care sacred isn't about calling on the right angel, or holding the right crystal . . . it's about having foundational self-care practices that you do consistently. They are non-negotiable and part of your healthy routine that's always prioritized. The vital importance of self-care is a lesson I have learned, and am often re-learning the hard way! So if you read this section and think, "Oh, wow, this is a strong reminder for me," I get it! Just head to the next exercise, and we'll get you back on track.

IDENTIFY FOUNDATIONAL SELF-CARE PRACTICES

STEP 1: Discern five of your top foundational self-care practices that have consistently worked well for you over time. The number five in numerology is an action-oriented number. These foundational self-care practices might include eating healthy, quality sleep, meditation, talk therapy, attending a weekly yoga class, taking supplements or medications, journaling, quality time with loved ones, feeling connected through volunteer work, massage, attending a weekly support-group meeting, relaxing quiet time or alone time, playing sports, playing music, making art, snuggling and cuddling, laughing and joking, spending time in nature, connecting with Spirit, cleaning and organizing, or pampering yourself.

STEP 2: For the next few weeks, make these foundational practices sacred. Remind yourself that they are non-negotiable, which means you might have to get creative about reminding yourself to do them or making space for them. You could even identify a self-care buddy and then help each other stay accountable—like walking the neighborhood together a few times every week. It can take three weeks, or twenty-one days, for a practice to become a habit.

STEP 3: Self-care should not be stressful! If you forget to do one of your foundational practices or really don't have time on a certain day, that's okay. Often clients will tell me in sessions that they know what self-care practices work for them, yet they go through long periods when they abandon these self-care practices. This exercise is merely meant to help you get back in the healthy rhythm of daily and weekly self-care.

> **MANTRA**
> My self-care practice doesn't have to be perfect. If I've gotten out of the habit of foundational self-care, I can be patient with myself as I rediscover my self-care rhythm. Basic self-care practices are the best way to protect myself as a sensitive person in the world.

HOW SENSITIVE ARE YOU TO COLLECTIVE ENERGY?

Your sensitivity and intuitive system are unique, which means you might be more sensitive to certain things than other sensitive people! I have a friend who is very sensitive to spirits, and can see ghosts—seeing ghosts with my physical eyes has only happened to me a handful of times. This friend is also very sensitive to rocks and crystals, so when I need a recommendation in that department, I know who to ask!

My sensitivity involves having all four psychic clairs active and open, which allows me to do such in-depth readings on clients. During my sessions with thousands of empath clients, I have occasionally met people who appeared to be more sensitive to collective energy than others. I hope this quiz will help you determine if you are particularly sensitive to collective energy.

Like anything, being more sensitive to collective energy has its blessings and its challenges. However you answer these questions has no bearing on whether you're a compassionate person. This quiz is simply trying to help you better understand your unique sensitivity.

Simply answer "very often" or "not often" to the following questions.

1. I really feel astrological cycles, like having lots of synchronicities during planetary shifts like Mercury retrograde or really feeling an energy shift in myself when the Moon is dark or full.

2. The changing seasons really affect my mood, like feeling more alive and energetic during spring and feeling more cozy and contemplative during winter. Sometimes

I can even sense the beginning of a new season before there is physical evidence of it yet.

3. When a big global event happens, I will sometimes realize that I felt anxious days beforehand, although—like the rest of the world—I had no idea what was coming.

4. When I learn about something happening in the world that has an intense energy signature—like a collective tragedy or a collective healing victory—it can affect my energy and mood significantly.

5. Even though it can sometimes be overwhelming and I have to temporarily pull back, I like to stay up on current events in my area and the world.

6. When something big is happening in the world or in my community, it's kind of on-and-off there in the background for me. It doesn't stop me from having my own unique emotions and experience, but at times it can inform them.

7. When there is a lot of celebration energy or grief energy collectively in my neighborhood, community, or country, I mindfully engage with it—but there also comes a point when I have to disengage from it just as mindfully.

8. As a child, when I heard about suffering in a distant part of the world, it was hard for me to take my mind off that suffering until a caring adult explained that this wasn't the best way to help others or myself. As an adult now, I'm learning that I may have to take my attention elsewhere when suffering in the world becomes all-consuming or too distracting for me.

9. Injustice of any kind has always bothered me, and can make me angry, sad, uncomfortable, and confused. Standing up for what seems fair, and for people who are being treated unfairly, is important to me.

10. When things are going well in my life, it automatically makes me want to spread the blessings around. While it's natural for people to want to share their blessings with loved ones and people they know well, I sometimes actually think of the people who are suffering most and how I might help them.

ANSWERED MOSTLY "VERY OFTEN":
As you probably suspected, it seems you might be very sensitive to collective energy. That's something you'll have to balance with being in your own energy and concerned with your own life. At different times in life, your focus on the collective will be lesser and greater, based in part on how much extra energy you have and what the current circumstances in your life are—as well as the circumstances in the world. Don't be afraid to pull back; and when it feels helpful and appropriate, don't be afraid to open up and feel. You'll be in a unique position to enjoy healing and celebratory energy when it hits the collective, letting it light you up! And when you're suffering, you might find ways to make your pain sacred to help the collective. That could look like training to become a health coach or nutritionist or physical therapist after you recover from a long healing journey, becoming an activist after a family member dies tragically, or using your creativity and story to inspire the world like singer/songwriter Nightbirde. Trust that you are sensitive to collective energy for a reason, and that in some way you might have a soul contract to work with or influence collective energy.

ANSWERED MOSTLY "NOT OFTEN":

Your answers would suggest that you're not as sensitive to collective energy; but while that may be true, there could be more to it. If you aren't as sensitive to collective energy now, remember that sensitivity and intuition are not static, so at another time in your life you might find you're suddenly much more sensitive to it! We can also numb out to collective energy as a protection mechanism, as we can all be so bombarded by global issues in the news and on social media. And sensitive people can go through burnout, just like other humans, where they simply don't have the emotional and physical reserves to care about things outside their very immediate circle. Sensitive empaths who are very compassionate going through burnout is something I cover in my book *Are You an Earth Angel?* So your lesser sensitivity to collective energy may be temporary. Or it could be a wonderful part of your magnificent, unique makeup. If you suspect that's the case, take a moment and think about what you might be exceptionally sensitive to—like animals or nature. Celebrate your unique sensitivity! I like to think we were all wired a certain way for a reason, so trust that your sensitivity and intuition are as they should be and best suited to not only your own journey but your unique relationship with the world.

Advice for all: When wanting to shield against challenging collective energy, try employing protective stones or symbols. I gave a friend dealing with a difficult manager the advice to place black obsidian on his desk, and remarkably that manager stopped approaching his desk! And a client who is sensitive to wandering spirits or ghosts has exceptional results with keeping spiritual symbols of protection that resonate with their beliefs around their home. (For more on helping lost spirits cross over, see my book *Angel Intuition*.) These techniques may or may not work with certain people or places, or in certain situations, but it's usually worth a try and can often be done discreetly.

Conclusion

Becoming Your Own Advocate

I f I could leave you with one parting bit of advice, from one sensitive to another, it would be to become your own advocate. With sensitive friends and family, sensitive clients, and myself, I have noticed a tendency among some empaths, at times, to have difficulty recognizing their power to champion themselves and own their journey. Being so sensitive to others can lead you to want to help others and thus forget to have your own back. As much as someone else you are in a relationship with wants the best for you, no one has your best interests at heart more than you do. This is your sacred territory and your sacred responsibility to yourself.

Being able to feel so much of the world outside yourself could make you sometimes feel small or insignificant, though nothing could be further from the truth. You are powerful, and you are most powerful when you are centered in your own energy and emotions and owning—at least the aspects you have some control over—your destiny. As you keep learning and evolving regarding how you show up to relationships as a sensitive person, remember to always show up for yourself, fight for yourself, love yourself, and hold yourself accountable in healthy ways.

In the first chapter of this book, we discussed using compassionate honesty as a communication style with others. You *can* tell others a hard or uncomfortable truth with love. Setting healthy boundaries with yourself and holding yourself accountable in a loving way is part of having your own back. Remember to be compassionately honest with yourself about your own journey.

If you enjoyed working with archangels in this book, try working with Archangel Ariel for better boundaries with yourself. This feminine-energy archangel reminds humans that we are each stronger, more capable, and more resilient than we realize, encouraging us to both ask for help from others (Archangel Ariel also rules abundance, and loves to assist humans with this) and to rely on *ourselves* during this human journey.

The journey of this book has been because of you! It's been informed by issues and experiences of sensitive people like you, and the publishing of this book was made possible by your direct support. Thank you, and take good, good care of yourself! You are needed in this world. Our time here is so very short—be *kind* to yourself.

With enormous gratitude and respect for you,

Tanya

Index

Note: Page numbers in *italics* indicate/include exercises and quizzes.

C

Cancer (zodiac sign), engaging with person born in, *206*

Capricorn, engaging with person born in, *208*

Cause, finding, *203*

Chakras
about, 12
on bottoms of feet, activating, 57
heart, connecting with, *22–23*
palm, feeling energy in, *18–19*
throat, nurturing, *12–14*

Chamuel, Archangel, 22

Changes, summoning courage to make, *68–69*

Child, giving yourself what you craved as, *55–56*

Chill energy, creating, *86–87*

Claim Your Sacred Clowns, *45*

Clairaudience, 111, 113, 114, *116*

Claircognizance, 24, 107, 111, 115, *116*, 123

Clairs (four), integrating, *111–117.* See also Clairaudience; Claircognizance; Clairsentience; Clairvoyance

Clairsentience
about, 10, 114–115
activating/playing with, 24, 114–115, *116–117*
art of compromise and, 10, 11
author's experience, 160
as one of the four clairs, 111–112, 113
relationships and, 106

Clairvoyance, 164
about, 115
author's experience, 113, 115
defined, 4
developing/playing with, 49, *116–117*
as one of the four clairs, 111–112, 113

Clutching, surrendering instead of, *59–62*

Cocoon to Calm, Release & Recenter, *82–83*

Come Home to Yourself, *61–62*

Communicating
admiration to others, 173
assistance from Archangel Gabriel, *11–12*
balancing energy exchanges and, 16–*19*
with compassionate honesty, *21–23*
confrontations and, *23–26*
empath talisman and, 16
empaths and, 2
heart chakra connection and, *22–23*
protection tips for observing, witnessing, 97 (See also Heart, protecting)
relationships and, 169–170, 171, 172, 173
telling others when feeling tender, *95–96*
when past wounds are triggered, 94–*96*
witnessing/observer mode and, *23–26*

Compassionate honesty, communicating with, *21–23*

Compile Your Relationship Rules, *171–172*

Compromise, art of, 8–*12*, 179

Confrontations, *23–26*

Connect With Star Energy, *77–78*

Connect with Your Heart Chakra Before Communicating, *21–22*

Coping skills, identifying, *122–123*

Create Chill Energy, *86–87*

Create Energy Instead of Mirroring It, *64–65*

Create Your Magical Healing Well, *51–53*

Crown Your Inner Sovereign, *3–4*

Crystal shop, lessons from, 194–195, 196

D

Depressants, 66

Dialogue with Your Inner Healer, *104*

About the Author

Tanya Carroll Richardson is an author, a professional intuitive, and a regular contributor to MindBodyGreen.com. Her nine nonfiction books include *Love Notes to My Self*, *Self-Care for Empaths*, *Are You an Earth Angel?*, *Angel Intuition*, *Forever in My Heart: A Grief Journal*, and *Zen Teen*. Tanya is also the author of the bestselling page-a-day calendar *A Year of Self-Love*. Follow her on social media at facebook.com /TanyaRichardsonBlessings and instagram.com/tanyacarrollrichardson, or sign up for Tanya's free newsletter by visiting tanyarichardson.com.

Also by Tanya Carroll Richardson:
Angel Insights (Llewellyn, 2016)
Angel Intuition (Llewellyn, 2018)
Are You an Earth Angel? (Llewellyn, 2020)
Awakening Intuition Oracle Deck (Insight Editions, Summer 2023)
Forever in My Heart: A Grief Journal (Ulysses Press, 2016)
Heaven on Earth (Sterling, 2015)
Love Notes to My Self (Workman/Hachette, 2022)
Self-Care for Empaths (Adams/Simon & Schuster, 2020)
A Year of Self-Love Page-a-Day Calendar (Workman/Hachette, annually)
Zen Teen (Seal Press/Hachette, 2018)